PRIVATE
REVOLUTIONS

PRIVATE REVOLUTIONS

Four Women Face
China's New Social Order

YUAN YANG

VIKING

VIKING
An imprint of Penguin Random House LLC
penguinrandomhouse.com

First published in hardcover in the United Kingdom by
Bloomsbury Publishing Plc, London, in 2024
First United States edition published by Viking, 2024

The poem "A Screw Fell to the Ground" by Xu Lizhi was translated by
friends of the Nao project and published on libcom.org.

LIBRARY OF CONGRESS CONTROL NUMBER: 2024016757
ISBN 9780593493908 (hardcover)
ISBN 9780593493915 (ebook)

Printed in the United States of America
1st Printing

Some names and identifying characteristics have been changed to protect
the privacy of the individuals involved.

致外公，外婆和老祖祖：你们教会了我如何讲故事。
致妈妈爸爸：因为你们，我才有故事可以讲。

For my maternal grandfather, grandmother and
great-grandmother, who taught me how to tell stories.

For *mama* and *baba*, who gave me a story to tell.

Guide to Names

The Chinese names in this book are written in the official *pinyin* system of romanised Mandarin Chinese that was invented by the Chinese Communist Party as part of its nation-building project in the 1950s. In Chinese, each character is one syllable. First names are usually one or two syllables, with equal stresses on each syllable.

Take note:
- Q = 'ch' as in 'cheese'
- X = 'sh' as in 'shush'
- Z = 'ds' as in 'reads'
- 'Zh' = this sound is sometimes taught to English speakers as 'r' as in 'work', but in southern Chinese accents, it is pronounced 'ds' as in 'reads'

Siyue: 'ss' (as in 'hiss') + 'y-weh'
Sulan, Siyue's mother: 'sue' + 'lan'
Guilan, Siyue's maternal grandmother: 'g-way' + 'lan'
Ziqiang, Siyue's uncle: 'ds' + 'ch-yang'
Jiaolong, the boy in Siyue's class: 'jow' (as in 'jowl') + 'long'
Jinghua, the girl in Siyue's dorm: 'jing' (rhymes with 'king') + 'h-wah'
Fanghui: 'f-ah-ng' + 'h-way'
Zijian, Siyue's father: 'ds' + 'j-yen'

June:
Gaolin: 'gow' (rhymes with 'wow') + 'lin'

Leiya: 'Lay' + 'yah'
Chufeng: 'choo' (as in 'choose') + 'fun-g'
Xinling: 'shin' + 'ling'
Guihua: 'g-way' + 'h-wah'
Yulan: 'y-wee' + 'lan'

Sam:
Zhao, Sam's mother: 'ds-ow' (rhymes with 'wow')
Zhou Xiuyun: 'ds-oh' ('oh' as in 'oath') 'show' + 'y-win'

Dan:
Yubin, Dan's grandmother: 'y-wee' + 'bin'

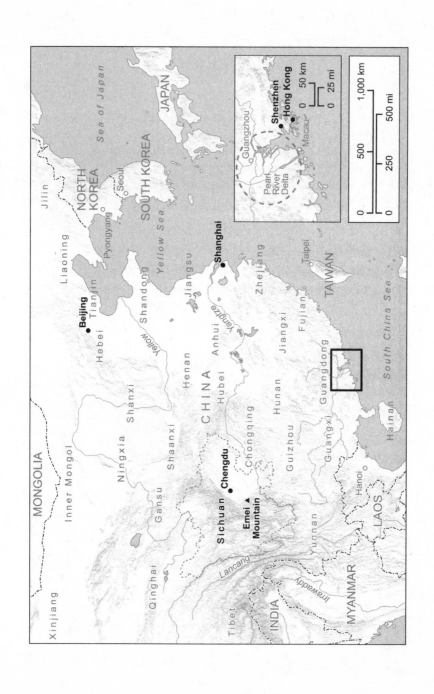

Preface

My maternal grandparents married in 1961, amid a man-made famine. On her wedding night, the bride walked home along streets shared by the bodies of the dead. Her colleagues had surprised her with an extravagant wedding gift – a handful of boiled sweets – which she held like gemstones in her pocket.

My parents were born after the harvests returned and began secondary school in the 1970s. At the start of each autumn term, my father would pay for his textbooks with barrowfuls of sweet potatoes. My paternal grandparents grew fields of the purple-skinned roots, which came into season in the early autumn and lasted throughout the winter.

My father had enough to eat, so long as what he wanted to eat was sweet potato. Every year, in the waning days of winter, he would get sick of their creamy caramel-orange hearts, the cloying mouthfeel that stuck no matter how they were cooked. He would start dreaming of the watermelon crop, two seasons away. But by the dog days of summer, sleeping with a hoard of watermelons under his bed, he would tire of their watery emptiness and long for sweet potatoes again.

I was born in 1990. One of my first words was *ga-ga*, the Sichuanese baby-talk for 'meat'. Every morning, my maternal great-grandmother would strap me to her back and walk down the hillside from my grandparents' apartment to the village market. She would run her fingers over the thick stems of asparagus lettuce, the fluffy pea shoots, the bumpy-skinned bitter gourds, naming each of them for me. I would wave my fat fist towards the red meat hanging from the butcher's hooks and say *ga-ga*.

My great-grandma would smile and buy the meat, and back home, she would proudly recount: *the little one said she wanted meat!*

———

In a country where the gap between rural and urban meant everything, I lived with my maternal grandparents in a place that straddled the two. It was a Communist work unit, or *danwei*, purposefully buried in the mountains of China's south-western interior to defend against potential attacks from the Soviet Union in the wake of the Sino-Soviet split of the early 1960s, when the two states' alliance broke down. In 1964, the government sent a team of engineers to Sichuan province to build the country's first semiconductor materials factory at the foothills of the holy Buddhist mountain of Emei. It was a tiny town planted into the countryside.

In the planned economy of the Mao era, the *danwei* did not only organise industrial production, but also provided a complete social infrastructure for workers to live within. My grandparents expected their *danwei* to take care of them, and it did.

Every weekday morning, we would wake around 6 a.m. to the sound of the loudspeakers playing the national anthem. An exodus of workers would make their way from the apartments on the hillside down to the factory near the village square. At lunchtime, they would go back home again to eat.

This job-for-life arrangement was called the 'iron rice bowl'. In my grandparents' factory, the rice was even steamed collectively. My grandfather would bring raw rice into the office in a tin lunch box, and place it between his many colleagues' lunch boxes in a metre-wide steaming pot. They would take the boxes home for lunch.

We had no running hot water at home, so to shower, the residents of the *danwei* would walk downhill past the factory gates and the ping-pong stadium to the communal showers. My grandpa would disappear into one doorway, and my grandma and I into another. At weekends, everyone had more time, and women and children congregated in the shower room, an open space without cubicle walls. The showerheads blasted bountiful hot water at high pressure, the steam billowing up the concrete walls. Children took small plastic buckets and toys for playing in the water. It had the atmosphere of a family outing, like going to the seaside.

Employees' children went to the primary school run by the *danwei*. It was much better than the rural schools nearby. Like the engineers who worked at the factory, the teachers of the *danwei* school were brought in from cities further afield.

In 1978, after Mao's death, Deng Xiaoping took over the Communist Party leadership and began capitalist reforms, beginning the era of 'Reform and Opening Up'. In the 1990s, the government rewrote the social contract. With the broader aim of instilling market competition and preparing China for accession to the World Trade Organization, the government started shutting down and privatising the old state-owned enterprises. In the decade after 1993, 50 million workers were laid off. Initially, the privatisation of the state enterprises was a free-for-all. Managers and local party bosses grabbed assets for themselves while leaving workers with nothing.

China experienced a wave of worker unrest. Many of these workers felt deeply betrayed by the state. Under the *danwei* system, they were a relatively privileged class: urban workers were accorded great respect under the Communist social order. Now they saw their *danweis* being ripped apart by financiers, party officials and managers, whose status was rising far above their own.

But by then, my grandparents were almost retired. Their factory, being of national technological importance, was kept in the arms of the state, and remained rich. They expected their *danwei* to take care of them, and it did.

———

On the other side of my family, my paternal grandparents were peasants. My father, who was born into rural poverty, knew he would do better than his parents, so long as he got off the sweet-potato farm. He got into a university on the other side of China, in my mother's south-western home province. My parents entered Sichuan University in 1981, becoming some of the first students to take up places at the newly reopened universities that Mao had closed during the Cultural Revolution. After they graduated in 1985, the government assigned them to teaching posts at a recently established university on the east coast.

I was born on that coastal campus. Shortly after, my mother moved to another Chinese university to pursue a doctorate in ancient history, while my father left for the UK to do the same in computer science. It was a simple decision for him: all the students who could leave were doing so. Chinese academia lagged behind the West, especially in the sciences, and the Beijing government's massacre of students and workers in Tiananmen Square in 1989 had left many questioning the future of China's universities. But neither of my parents was capable of taking a baby with them. Before my first birthday, my great-grandma took me on the two-day train ride to Emei Mountain, to live with her and my grandparents.

My grandfather had never taken care of an infant before I arrived, because he himself had left home to work in the city of Chengdu, Sichuan's provincial capital, when my mother was small. But he discovered by chance that when I cried in the middle of the night for my mother's milk, he could calm me down by telling me stories. After many months of this, I started telling him stories back. They featured me, my grandma and grandpa.

When I turned four, my parents plucked me from my home in the Sichuanese mountains and took me to England. In the photo of me leaving my grandparents at the departures gate in Beijing Capital Airport, my grandma stands next to my grandpa, who is holding me in his arms while I cling on to his grey shirt. The three of us look dismayed, rather than excited, about my journey to a place with many more opportunities than a small town in Sichuan.

From then on, I only visited China in the summer holidays, when I went on the pilgrimage back to my grandparents' home. The whole country to me was encompassed by the smell of white gardenias growing in my grandparents' vegetable patch, the feel of the wet heat of the south-western Chinese summer. Nothing seemed to change in my grandparents' *danwei* until I turned eighteen, when a tarmac road unfurled from it to Emei's town centre.

––––

This was the China I knew before I returned to live there in 2016 as a journalist for the *Financial Times*. My impetus to return to the country partly came from a desire to immerse myself in the language. I had studied economics with a focus on developing countries, thinking I would work on the problems of poverty, but what we learned in the classroom was far removed from what happened on the ground. I wanted to be there. My parents were supportive: my mother, who had studied ancient Chinese literature and history, had always wanted me to connect to the culture that had been her passion.

I moved to the arid northern capital of Beijing, and finally, in my mid-twenties, came to know China on my own terms. I booked my own long-distance trains, no longer being shuttled around like a piece of luggage like I had as a child.

Before I went back to China, I knew the optimistic giddiness of my parents' generation, where they could expect to out-earn their parents no matter what, so long as they got out of the village. When I arrived, I found the onset of now-pervasive class anxieties. There was the fear of rural families that the gap between them and urban families had widened so much that their children would find it difficult to make it in the city. And there was the fear of well-off urban parents that their wealth came from luck and timing and an unrepeatable economic boom, and their children would struggle to have the same fortune.

A friend of mine calls this latter worry the fear of 'falling off the ladder'. Over the past three decades, the ladder has grown very tall.

———

In my first summer in Beijing, I was at a rooftop party when a young woman tapped me on the shoulder.

'Hello,' she said, 'I couldn't help overhearing your conversation. You speak with a bit of a Sichuanese accent. I'm from Sichuan! And you sound like you're a journalist. I'm a journalist, too!'

Thus began my friendship with Dan. Later, she would tell me that I had looked so desperately naive about the ways of China's big cities that she had felt the need to intervene. She, too, had once been a newcomer in a city. And she resented that city for barring her from calling it home.

Like me, Dan was born in 1990. Like mine, her parents also pursued their dreams in a faraway place: for them, it was the up-and-coming southern coastal city of Shenzhen. They joined the hundreds of millions of migrant workers who left the countryside every year to make a living in the cities, where they could earn several times what they made on their farms.

So Dan and I were left with our maternal grandparents in Sichuan. This was very normal at the time, and is only slightly less so now. It made us technically part of the vast class of 'left-behind children' created by migration to cities. The term is synonymous with educational disadvantage and emotional abandonment. But Dan and I were both lucky not to experience it that way: we were the centre of the world to our grandparents. My great-grandma stayed at home and would cook for us all, narrating each step of the recipe to me in her continuous Sichuanese patter long before I could speak; when my grandparents came home from the factory, they loved to make up stories to tell me.

Just before we started school, our parents took us away again. Dan's parents brought her to Shenzhen. Sitting sandwiched on the train between the uncles who were taking her away from her grandparents was the first time she ever recalled feeling lonely.

I learned to speak English. Dan learned to speak standard Mandarin, rather than the Sichuanese dialect she had grown up with. Through luck and family connections, she managed to get a place at a state-run city school.

Initially, Dan didn't think about the differences between her and her classmates, almost all of whom had been raised by urban families in Shenzhen. She started to wonder during middle school, when she was given a form for her parents to fill in that required them to list their occupations.

By then, Dan's father was working as a bike mechanic, operating out of a cart by the side of the road. Looking at the form, he hesitated for a long time before finally writing: 'Sole trader'. Dan felt the label didn't quite fit. *To be a sole trader, don't you need to at least own a shop?* she thought.

Soon she started hiding her family's circumstances from her classmates. This was particularly difficult because her father's bike-mechanic cart was always parked on the side of a street that her classmates sometimes passed by after school. He often pumped their tyres without revealing who he was; he didn't want to embarrass Dan. She never brought school friends home to the cramped apartment they shared with two other families.

In her early teens, Dan was forced to leave the city. It turned out to be easier for my parents to become British nationals a decade after arriving in the UK than it was for Dan's parents to change their rural *hukou* – the household registration that divides China into geographical classes – into a Shenzhen city *hukou*. A *hukou* determines where you can go to school, access public health care, and other government services; it used to dictate where you could live and work, and still conditions where you can buy property.

A year after I became British, Dan had to go back to Sichuan. Her luck with the school system had run out. Even though she was always near the top of her class at her middle school, she needed a Shenzhen *hukou* in order to take the university entrance exams in the city.

At the age of fourteen, she left Shenzhen and started school in the town nearest her family's village, which was still a full day's travel away from her grandparents. Dan went to live in a dormitory at her new school. She learned to stop speaking in standard Mandarin, and went back to Sichuanese.

––––

Hearing Dan's story caused me to reflect on what might have happened had my parents remained in China. If they hadn't left for the UK, my parents could have stayed in the coastal city where I was born, in Ningbo. I could have grown up learning how to crack snow crabs from their crusts. I would have been part of China's first major wave of children born into urban prosperity, raised with expectations of continuous rise. But by the late 2000s, when I was ready to take the entrance exams for university, I would have been competing with over 10 million high-school-educated children across China, rather than the 3 million that my parents were up against.

Maybe I would have got into a Beijing university and settled in the capital. My parents would own the flat their *danwei* had assigned them in Ningbo, but the value of a flat in a third-tier city would be nowhere near enough to help me settle down in Beijing. Back in the UK, my friends shut out of London call themselves 'Generation Rent'. My friends in Beijing are 'Generation Involution': the term, taken from anthroplogy, has recently become popular in China, and means a system which absorbs ever more effort for ever less return.

––––

The more I spoke to my friends about their perceptions of social mobility in China today, the more stories I heard of women whose paths to the big city had been long and winding, and who had to remake themselves over and over. I began to look for women whose stories exemplified the changes in the Chinese economy over the past thirty years, who could speak to what it felt like to live through such rapid dislocation. News journalism usually sees economic shifts at the scale of a whole country; I wanted to write at the scale of an individual's interior life.

This book is about revolutions in two senses. It is about China's economic revolution from the 1980s and 90s onwards, after the Reform and Opening Up era, when private enterprise became legal and state planning was partially replaced with market mechanisms.

It is also about the personal revolutions undertaken by four young women born in those decades as they came of age amid the inconsistent rise – and now stumble – of social mobility in China's capitalist era. Leiya, born in a patriarchal rural village, wants to escape a gendered destiny where she is only seen as useful for bearing sons. June, born in a remote mountain village, has her curiosity sparked by a chance meeting with a teacher from afar. Siyue, born to rural entrepreneurs, rebels against her teachers in school, and then remakes the education system for others. And Sam, born to urban middle-class parents, is inspired by the Marxist revolutionaries who founded modern China, and wants to recreate their legacy.

My stories are centred around women who still mainly carry the social role of producing and shaping the next generation. This means they exemplify China's transformations on many levels: in schools, in factories and in the home.

But I also write about women because I found that women were more willing to open up to me – an interviewer and friend of similar age, gender and ethnicity – about the intimate transformations that accompanied the social and economic shifts in their lives. Over the course of my six years of reporting in China, my interviewees took me into their homes. I saw what is passed on from grandmother to mother to daughter, what is lost, and what is invented afresh. I am incredibly grateful to them for entrusting me with their stories.

Since the mid-2010s, deepening political repression and censorship has made it ever more difficult to gain intimate access to Chinese interviewees. I feel glad to have been in China just before the door to the outside world started closing. Local government and police interference, or the threat of it, stopped me from speaking to many more people.

We are entering an era in Chinese politics where sensitivities are increasingly unpredictable and arbitrary, where what was acceptable yesterday becomes unexpectedly dangerous today. The state surveillance and propaganda systems are not only built to repress stories that might challenge the regime, they are now built to repress nearly all stories, whether they show the darkness or the light of life in China.

In an effort to protect my interviewees from state harassment, I have anonymised them to the extent possible, and changed non-historical dates and the names of certain locations. I have removed many details I would have wished to include. Their stories, however, speak for themselves.

I do not believe in an inevitable march from poverty to progress. Life gets worse and better for different groups in different ways. The diversity of stages of economic development within China means that its problems are a microcosm of the world's. China's urban–rural divide has grown wide enough that its big cities exemplify the urban problems of the global north, while its rural villages still retain the problems of the global south. Meanwhile, rich economies like those of the US and UK have also become more dualistic, with a widening gap between winners and losers.

Any mass transformation of society requires, and results in, massive change at the level of individuals, friendships and families. Yet it is also easy, at a time of such breakneck change, to lose sight of what it feels like to be alive. The four women in this book show us how we both create and are recreated by societal changes. I hold up their stories as a mirror to our own.

Part One

I

The riverside
Siyue

Guide to Chinese school grades: primary school begins at age six, middle school ('lower-secondary') at age twelve; those who go on to high school ('upper-secondary') do so at fifteen; university begins at eighteen.

———

It would always be on the phone to her mother that Siyue felt the most criticised. Siyue lived in the village with her grandma, who had no phone line, so she would go next door to use the neighbour's phone to speak to her mother. The receiver was a little big for her head, and the heat of her mother's voice would radiate from it, blazing with scorn, until Siyue couldn't help but cry, sobbing shamefully in her neighbour's living room.

Siyue was not doing well at primary school. She was the kind of eight-year-old who liked to daydream more than she liked to memorise. She didn't find it easy to sit still, and when she got home, she rarely did her homework. In truth, she barely remembered enough from the day to even know what homework she was meant to be doing. She argued fiercely with her teachers, once shredding an entire schoolbook page by page in the middle of class.

Teachers mistrusted her. She was best at Chinese, and loved to write, but her Chinese teacher bore a grudge against her. Once, after Siyue won a school essay-writing contest, her teacher reacted to the news by raising her eyebrows, walking into the corridor, and tearing her essay off the wall display.

Siyue's mother knew her maths teacher, and routinely showered her with small gifts, as one does to get one's child some extra attention in a class with fifty students. But it didn't help much. After Siyue did well on a maths test, her teacher asked her who she had copied from. Siyue expressed her anger towards her teacher by refusing to care about maths. In her next exam, she wandered out of the classroom after ten minutes. That had earned her a 10 per cent, which had led to the phone call.

Siyue was three years younger than the other kids in her class. Her parents had used their connections in the village to get her into school early. Doing so made things easier for her grandma, who was taking care of her while her parents were living and working far from the village. That was one of the benefits of a village school: it was easy to relax the rules. Siyue's mother had also noticed she had started reading earlier than her peers and hoped she might become a promising student.

Her mother's hopes were short-lived. As a child, Siyue had a short attention span. At the start of her second year of primary school, her parents had transferred her to a school in the town. In her third year, she had moved to another campus, with new teachers. She started feeling immobilised by the fear of making a mistake whenever she was called up to the front of class. In her fourth year, she was sent to another village school near her paternal grandparents, with a completely different teaching style from the town school. In her fifth year, she moved again, back to her maternal grandma's village. Five schools in five years.

————

The home Siyue liked most was her maternal grandma Guilan's, a farmhouse in a traditional four-walled courtyard. One of her grandma's rooms was filled with books – a rarity in the village. It was stocked with the books Siyue's aunt had read at university, as well as Siyue's mother's old novels.

As befitting the Chinese stereotype of doting elders, Siyue's grandparents went easy on her compared to her parents. Siyue's grandfather had missed out on the childhoods of his own children, since he had also spent the prime of his life far from the village, working in the city. Their village was near the east coast of China, on a tributary of the Yangtze River that flows to Shanghai. In 1950, when he was sixteen, Siyue's grandfather had taken a boat down that river to find work in the city. He only returned to the village, briefly, in order to get married.

Siyue's grandma had raised her daughters mostly on her own. She was illiterate, and had made it her priority to put her children through school. When her husband was away in the city and wrote her letters, she had to ask others in the village to help her read them and to write back to him. Guilan resented her illiteracy for denying her privacy with her own husband. Her eldest daughter, Siyue's mother Sulan, was one of the very few children in her village to get into high school. The three extra years she spent there meant three years of forgone wages for the household. After not getting into university on her first attempt, Guilan encouraged her to try again, but Sulan was too cowed by the idea of costing her family another year of lost wages.

By the time Siyue was born in the late 1980s, her grandfather was comfortably retired. He was one of the only men in the village with a pension, because he had once worked at a state-owned factory. Unlike the other grandparents, he didn't need to worry about money or farm work; he spent every month's pension on the best food for his grandchildren, knowing there would always be more money next month.

Siyue saw her grandfather as the kitchen magician, someone who could conjure up sweetness from nowhere. He kept hidden in the house a hemp sack of tiny honey tangerines, and would bring a few out for Siyue when she was in a bad mood. When he discovered how much she liked strawberries, he cleared out his vegetable patch and planted it over with them. In the hot summers, he made her cold snacks of his invention by filling a metal pot with sugar-studded cucumbers and lowering it into the dark depths of their well. In the winters, he'd rise before her, set the breakfast pot bubbling on the stove, and then wake her by asking her to go and see what was in the pot.

There was always meat on the table – a luxury in the village. Siyue's grandfather liked to spoil his grandchildren with the food he hadn't eaten in his own childhood. When Siyue's cousin came to visit, he would buy a whole chicken, chop it into chunks, and braise it with caramelised sugar and soy sauce. He always added extra sugar. Siyue loved stewed pork, river shrimp and the fish her grandfather caught from the local streams. Her grandfather often took her to the riverside to go fishing, and he'd bring their elderly ginger-and-white cat along too, holding the dozing cat in his arms while Siyue held one of its paws.

Her parents didn't know the meaning of taking it easy. They flitted between their village and other cities – wherever their entrepreneurial experiments took them.

In the 1980s, Siyue's parents had been one of the first to dive 'into the sea', the term used for the risk-takers who set up businesses during the early days of China's market opening. Like other eastern villages near Shanghai, Siyue's was being enriched by the policy of Reform and Opening Up. In the 1990s, relatives of traders in Shanghai started bringing home piecework for the women of the village to do. Weaving together hammocks for foreign buyers earned Siyue's grandmother vastly more money than farming, and the village's wealth started to grow, as well as villagers' expectations of a better life.

But with expectation came comparison and jealousy. Siyue's father had been one of the first in their village to register himself as a sole trader. An electrical engineer by training, he'd run the repairs department of a state-owned department store in the nearby town during the planned economy of the 1970s. On the side, he repaired radios himself, setting up a stall through the window of his house, which opened onto the street. As soon as he was allowed to open a private business after the market reforms of the 1980s, he did so. Riches and new contraptions poured into the house. When the village matchmaker first took Siyue's mother to his home on a winter evening, she was amazed by the blaze of electric lights radiating from within. There was a television aerial on the roof, a twenty-inch television in the living room, and a washing machine in the kitchen. It was the first time she had seen such things.

Siyue's mother joined her new husband's business, and they became a formidable pair. They opened several factories along the eastern coast for manufacturing and repairing electronics. Business was so good that Sulan's hands would get sore from counting out all the ten-renminbi notes. At the end of each day, she would stuff the notes into large hemp sacks and haul them to the bank. Soon the bank was sending staff to her house every day to help with the counting.

The local officials, who had not gone 'into the sea' but were instead drying out in the state system, got wind of Siyue's parents' profits. Siyue's father refused on principle to give them anything extra to smooth the relationship; they accused him of not paying enough tax, and he appealed the case in court. Ever since Siyue could remember, her parents would have tense arguments at home about their business. She didn't understand the details as a child, but they were locked in a series of lawsuits with the local government, and spent most of their vast earnings fighting them. The threats they received escalated; at one point the local officials cut off the electricity supply to their house, plunging them into darkness. Sulan sometimes wondered if she should send Siyue to a more distant relative in another village for safekeeping in case the officials became more menacing.

Siyue, however, felt safe in her village, and liked to wander alone down the paths between seemingly endless fields, surrounded by neighbours she knew well. The paths turned into bridges over willow-lined brooks that criss-crossed the land, creating the watery southern Chinese scenery celebrated by the nation's poets.

Once, when Siyue's grandma was a teenager, she ran away from her stepmother and took a boat down to Shanghai. But there was no river that could take Siyue away from her mother's ire.

Nor did Siyue's mother feel she had any channel to get through to her daughter. During Siyue's fifth year of primary school, her mother came home, and took her to the riverside.

'Do you want to die?' her mother said, standing with her on the bank above the river, in whose currents floated the tangled hair of its weeds. 'Why don't you go and die right now? Your grades are this bad, why don't you just die?'

———

Siyue's mother raised her the same way she herself had been raised, the way her sisters and brothers raised their kids. Her parenting role model was her brother-in-law Ziqiang, a stocky army man who could send a child halfway across a room with one blow. He would brag about how well his son was doing at school and how he had instilled discipline through beatings, while the other kids in his military compound got into scrapes with the police. If you didn't beat a child, he argued, they would go bad. If they went bad, they wouldn't do well in school, and then they would be destined for a life of farm labour. If you didn't beat your child, life would knock them down.

Siyue's parents approved of the intention behind Ziqiang's beatings, but they never beat Siyue. Her mother had wanted to scare her by taking her to the riverside, to shock her into reconsidering her life. It didn't work: Siyue had been scolded enough to have developed immunity. She was in a cycle of vicious rebellion with her parents. The more she was told off, the more ingenious ways she'd find to misbehave.

It couldn't go on like this. After Siyue finished primary school, her parents decided to bring her to Shenzhen, where the schools were better and they could keep a closer eye on her.

Siyue had liked Shenzhen when she had visited back when her father was doing a stint as the interim chief executive officer of a friend's property business, having been forced to wrap up his electronics business. He had had a company driver take her around the city.

Those were the days her parents had seemed most relaxed, her mother always wearing something beautiful. On one of Siyue's trips, her mother had gifted her a watch with a gold-coloured face. Back in the village primary school, she would daydream and gaze into the watch's face, imagining it was the landscape of a vast city, an outside that she was desperate to see.

But the golden days didn't last for long. Just before Siyue moved to Shenzhen for middle school in 1997, her parents started another business, selling and repairing Nokia mobile phone handsets. They had a small shopfront in Shenzhen's sprawling Huaqiangbei market, which remains to this day the world's biggest electronics wholesale market. But although they didn't sell fakes themselves, they got caught up in the crackdowns on counterfeit goods that could close the market for weeks at a time. Money became tight again. Siyue's parents took out their stress on the easiest target: Siyue's poor school record.

In Siyue's mind, her family's finances and her grades twisted into one dark omen looming over her. 'If you don't study properly, then there's no hope,' her parents would scold her. 'In two months, we'll be out on the street, sleeping under the bridge.'

Siyue's family didn't have a Shenzhen *hukou*, which meant that it would be very difficult for Siyue to enrol directly in a Shenzhen middle school. While she was finishing primary school back home, her parents started building their case. They rented a flat next door to a good state school. Then they started inviting friends of friends who worked for the Education Bureau out for dinner, trying to find someone who might be able to loosen the restrictions for them. The restaurant bills were stacking up, but nobody had the right strings to pull. Two days before the start of the new school year, Siyue's parents spent the entire day in taxis, frantically zipping across Shenzhen trying to find someone who could help them in the little time they had left.

By the time term started, Siyue still didn't have a school place. Sulan went to speak directly to the headmaster at the school next door. She presented her story: her daughter was already living with them in Shenzhen, and it wasn't easy for them, coming out to work so far from their home town. He listened patiently but didn't give any ground. 'It's not easy for many people,' he said. 'I can't make an exception just for you.'

Still, Sulan interpreted the headmaster's gentleness as the sign of a kind heart. For the next three days she turned up at the end of school, went to his office, swept his floor, and poured him tea. When she left the room, she walked backwards in order to face him, the palms of her hands pressed together at her chest in supplication.

'Please stop coming,' he told her. 'I can't do anything for your daughter.'

On the fourth day, when the situation seemed hopeless, Sulan's luck finally kicked in: a family friend had found an Education Bureau official who could write her a note ordering the school to accept Siyue. But just as Sulan was leaving the bureau with the note, the official's secretary ran after her.

'A word of advice,' she said. 'The headmaster you spoke to isn't from here. He won't be swayed by pressure from local officials. In fact, it might get his back up. He's a principled man. I suggest you try speaking to him again before sending the note.'

Sulan turned up at the headmaster's office one last time. She explained that since term had started, Siyue had already lost her school place back in her home town, and this was her only chance to study. With every word she spoke, she carefully watched the headmaster's face; she stopped or changed tack immediately if she saw she was losing him. Finally, he told her to bring Siyue in the next day to take an entrance exam.

———

At first, Siyue didn't understand what anyone was saying at her new school. Although the official language of instruction was standard Mandarin, the teachers and the kids often spoke to one another in Cantonese, the southern Chinese dialect of Guangdong province and Hong Kong that is arguably a language unto itself.

But even after she learned how to speak Cantonese, she didn't know what to say. The Shenzhen girls had much more mature tastes than the twelve-year-olds in Siyue's village. They laughed at Siyue's Mickey Mouse backpack. They picked their own clothes, which changed frequently. They wore their hair in asymmetrical cuts, and went out to bars at the weekends. Their parents were wealthy because they owned houses in the city. Studying would not make or break their futures.

The school curriculum was also entirely different. Shenzhen's curriculum remained heavily influenced by its formerly colonised neighbour, Hong Kong. Kids in Shenzhen started learning English in primary school, but back in Siyue's village, they only started in middle school.

Siyue knew not to talk to her parents about her problems making friends: they would tell her she was at school to learn, not to socialise. Eventually, she learned to drag her desk into the teachers' office during lunchtime so that the other kids wouldn't leave dead bugs inside it. After a while she made one good friend, another outsider: a girl who had moved from another town.

Siyue grew to like her teachers, who were smart and had needed high qualifications in order to work in Shenzhen. She loved the after-school activities – the school put on storytelling competitions, music classes and art workshops as part of a new emphasis on holistic education in China's modern cities. One term, Siyue became the anchor for the school radio, and went in early once a week to read the news. Another term, she worked for the school library; she felt trusted and respected by the teachers when they gave her the keys to the place. But back at home, Siyue felt trapped in cycles of hurt with her parents, neither understood nor respected.

Throughout Siyue's school years, reading was her escape. At the weekends, she received a few renminbi from her mother to go to the Shenzhen Book City, a three-storey bookshop in the city centre. Siyue would walk and save the bus fare in order to buy herself a sweet bun from the bookshop's Cantonese bakery, the kind covered with a crunchy yellow-sugar crust that resembled the skin of a pineapple. She would eat the bun for lunch, then settle back into reading on the floor of the bookshop, where she could happily spend the rest of the day.

Siyue liked reading English literature in translation: her favourite book was *Jane Eyre*. She understood it as a story about a heroine who is plain and poor, yet bold, who is in love with a man of higher status. She memorised one of Jane's speeches to Mr Rochester:

Do you think, because I am poor, obscure, plain, and
little, I am soulless and heartless? You think wrong! –
I have as much soul as you – and full as much heart! And
if God had gifted me with some beauty and much wealth,
I should have made it as hard for you to leave me, as it
is now for me to leave you. I am not talking to you now
through the medium of custom, conventionalities, nor
even of mortal flesh: it is my spirit that addresses your
spirit; just as if both had passed through the grave, and we
stood at God's feet, equal – as we are!

She liked to bring home romance novels from her school
library. The women in them were powerless and beautiful,
the plots silly and fantastical. She'd read them in her bedroom
with the door locked. If she forgot to lock the door, her mother
might catch her reading and fly into a rage, snatching the
book away and throwing it back at her. Once, in a particularly
intense rage, her mother ripped the book up page by page and
threw the scraps out the window. 'If you read books like this,'
she yelled, 'you'll become a bad person.'

Siyue missed her grandparents. For her three whole years
of middle school, her parents didn't once go back to her
grandparents' village. Siyue would call them from her parents'
apartment in the city and, hearing their voices on the other
end of the distant line, she'd start to cry.

———

In Siyue's second year of middle school, her parents' finances
became less precarious, their Nokia mobile-handset business
bringing in thousands of renminbi every day. Still, it was much
smaller in scale than their old electronics-repair business back
in the village, because they had few savings left to invest after
the government lawsuits. Siyue's mother suspects it was the

yearning for what he had lost that drove Siyue's father to the stock markets.

Closed for over forty years after the Communist Revolution of 1949, Shanghai's stock exchange was re-established in November 1990, and a few days later, Shenzhen set up its own stock exchange too. In the mid-2000s, a surge of amateur investors opened accounts. China's stock markets are still dominated by household investors who make their own decisions rather than handing their money over to financial institutions. To this day, Chinese families have internationally high levels of savings, and few options for good investments outside of the property market.

The idea that fortunes could be made or destroyed overnight on the stock market made sense to a generation that came of age in the 1980s and 90s, the growth-spurt decades of the Reform and Opening Up era, when riches seemed to randomly fall into the laps of one's neighbours. The same mindset also made those left behind by the market reforms vulnerable to pyramid schemers and fraudsters. In search of the wild success that had been taken away from him by the jealous officials of his home town, Siyue's father bet the family savings – which were around Rmb1 million – on the stock market.

At the end of her three years in middle school, Siyue passed the entrance exams for a Shenzhen high school. But there was no point in going. Siyue's *hukou* was still tied to her riverside birthplace, almost 1,000 miles north of Shenzhen. Without a Shenzhen *hukou*, she found herself in a similar situation to Dan: she would not be allowed to take the university entrance exams in Shenzhen. Since the exam format and curriculum varied from province to province, her parents sent Siyue back home for high school, where she would be able to prepare for the university exams of her home province.

Through their local connections, Siyue's parents secured her a place at one of the best high schools in the small city near their home town. Like most of the students, who were drawn from a wide catchment of surrounding villages, Siyue lived in the school dorms. Her four dorm-mates were all scholarship girls from the farmland: studying was their ticket out of poverty, and they were extremely good at it. They were the kind of girls who studied from the moment they got up in the morning to after lights-out at 9 p.m., reading with a light underneath their duvets.

On her first day of high school, Siyue entered her new classroom in a white cotton dress, only to be faced with rows of students in sweatpants. She had spent enough time in Shenzhen to have taken on the fashions of the city girls. But, unlike in middle school, the home-town kids didn't bully her. In general, they ignored her. They had all gotten where they were through well-practised studying for tests; they were too focused on work to have any time for anything else.

Across China, every student taking the *gaokao*, the formidable university entrance exam, starts with vastly different educational resources, but everyone has the same number of hours in the day to beat to a pulp. To compete with the city kids, the small-town kids have to cram harder. Like many small-town schools, Siyue's taught its students to spend long hours filling in multiple-choice practice tests.

This approach was at odds with the methods in Siyue's Shenzhen school, which had offered the extra-curricular activities like radio broadcasting and public speaking that Siyue had so enjoyed. Back in her home-town high school, Siyue sat through non-stop lectures, getting lost in the stream of words.

One evening towards the end of her second year of high school, Siyue was reviewing English homework with a friend, when the friend suddenly turned to her.

'Is your English really that bad?' her friend said.

Siyue felt that familiar rush of shame, the feeling that had dogged her since her first days of primary school. It started in the solar plexus, a hollowness that spread to the heart.

Her friend's comment wasn't baseless: Siyue had recently come second to last in her class for English. When she got home, she resolved to put all her effort into studying it.

She liked the subject, but had struggled to keep up with the fast-paced English curriculum at her Shenzhen school, where the local kids had started studying the language several years before her. She liked reading English books in translation, like Jane Eyre, and thought of learning a foreign language as opening a window to somewhere glimmering and full of possibility, somewhere less suffocating than her home. She dedicated the summer holiday to teaching herself English. There was no beauty in the way the school taught English, Siyue thought: it was all fill-in-the-blank worksheets and tick-box grammar tests.

So, Siyue designed her own English classes. Every morning of the summer holiday, she got up and read English phrases out loud into a voice recorder, and then played them back to herself. On her Walkman CD player, she listened to English-language programmes, then stopped the CD, and repeated the lines. She was a natural impersonator.

Two months went by, and she realised she was neither stupid nor bad at studying: she simply didn't suit rote-teaching. Her English scores improved far more after a summer of independent study than they had in years of drilling from her teachers. In her first English test of the new school year, she came top of her class. But by then, it was almost too late to turn all of her grades around. Her university entrance exams were almost upon her.

2

The path-breakers
June

Chinese geographical administrative divisions: hamlet (smallest) < village < township < county town < city (biggest)

When June saw her mother's body, her white teeth were visible under lips caked in black dust. The white bones of her ankles, too, had had their skin scraped open by the rocks of coal that had crushed her.

It was the spring of 2009 and June was thirteen years old. She was finishing her first year of middle school in the county town a day's walk from her village in the mountains of southern China. Several years earlier, her mother had gone to work at a coal mine far from the province. She had been the family's main breadwinner; June's father worked on the farm at home. Her mother had arranged for June to stay with a friend in the county town and go to middle school there, because she was worried she would be led astray by the kids in their local township school, half of whom would eventually drop out.

June's first venture into the county town had brought out her experimental side: skipping classes, singing at karaoke bars and testing the patience of her mother's friend by coming home at midnight. During this wild-child period, her five-years-older sister, May, who could be proud and icy at times, had briefly refused to speak to her. But June had wanted to experience everything the town could offer.

A few days before she was crushed on the conveyor belt at the mine, June's mother had sent June her monthly allowance and called her on the phone. 'Study hard,' she had reminded her, 'especially since your dad won't be able to earn much, the way he is now.'

Then, her mother was gone. June prepared to leave the county town to move back to live with her father and grandma to save money. Her middle-school teachers, who had marked her down as a future dropout, didn't ask what had happened.

Taking the day-long bus with her uncles and sister to identify her mother's body at the mine, a couple of hundred miles away, was the first time June had ever left her home province. On the way there, the adults wept, but the whole episode seemed unreal to June and her sister. Her mother had been working far from home since June was little. June idolised her. When her mother came back during the harvest seasons, before June was old enough to be of help, she would sit in the fields, watching her, not wanting her to leave.

When she drew back the curtain on her mother's body, she was struck by the immensity of what had been taken from her. On the way home, June finally cried. She felt herself on the verge of a new and unknown life.

––––

Her mother's death wasn't June's first encounter with her parents' mortality. Three years earlier, when she was ten years old, June had saved her father's life.

That year, her mother was home for the first long stretch that June could remember, helping June's father build their new house by the side of the path into the village. They had borrowed money to buy the bricks and concrete.

Their old home had been made of branches and thatch, like most houses in the village. One winter when it hailed, balls of ice rained into their bedroom and they took shelter in the pigsty on the ground floor, which was covered over with wooden planks.

Back then, her sister was finishing middle school, and was only home at weekends. A boy in the village had started following May around. He acted like he was her rightful boyfriend. One afternoon, while June's uncles were visiting, the boy walked straight into their home and into May's bedroom, where she was napping. The uncles beat him up and threw him out.

A few days later, when only June's father was home, the boy walked back into the house with a knife. The rest of the family was at a wedding; June's father had come back early and was sorting out the boxes of leftovers from the feast. Seeing the boy, her father raised his arm to defend himself. When June came back home with her grandma shortly after, she found him slumped on the floor, his right arm slashed open by the knife, his intestines hanging out of a gash in his belly.

Her grandma, who always expected and prepared for the worst, told June to put her father's living body in the dried hay, as they had no coffin prepared. Her own husband had died young; so had her father, June's great-grandfather.

June started crying. Apart from her grandma and injured father, she was the only one home: her uncles and other relatives were still at the wedding party. In the dark evening, June ran through the village shouting for help.

The adults came back home with her, but stood outside the front door, wailing as if at a funeral. In the chaos, June remembered her primary-school teacher telling them about '120', the phone number you were meant to dial for medical emergencies. With both of her parents having toiled in distant cities at different points, they were privileged to have a fixed-line phone, which was often borrowed by the other families of their hamlet.

June dialled 120. It was the first call she had made to an outside world that she had barely seen; she wasn't sure if anyone would pick up, but they did. She described to the stranger on the other end the rocky path that led to their village. Eventually, the ambulance arrived at the bottom of the path, unable to drive up. The adults laid her dad on a wooden door atop a ladder and carried him the three hours' walk down to the main road. He was still alive, but barely.

Her uncles went to the boy's house the same night, but hadn't found him. After accompanying June's father to hospital, they went back to their own village, several hours' walk away from June's. A few days after the stabbing, her uncles called her, and asked her to check the boy's house to see if there was anyone home. June went to look, and saw smoke coming through the chimney. She called her uncles, who found the boy and took him to the police. June could take on anyone.

Her mother came home to visit her father in hospital. By then his condition had stabilised, and he had been transferred to the county-town hospital, because their local township hospital didn't have the expertise to treat him. Though the township hospital felt expensive, the county-town hospital was enough to bankrupt a family.

On the road opposite the hospital two girls were begging. Her mother crossed over to give them Rmb10, a month's living expenses. When she came back, tears were welling up in her eyes.

'Why did you do that?' June asked. 'Why give money away when we're in so much debt?'

'Those two reminded me of you and your sister,' her mother replied. 'When your father first went into hospital and we thought he might die, I thought that's what we'd have to do with you two.'

When June's father left hospital, he had little strength in his right arm, but could still do some forms of manual labour. Her mother went to work in the coal mine to pay off the tens of thousands of renminbi they had accumulated in debt for the new house and the medical bills. At the time, June couldn't have imagined how the near loss of one of her parents' lives would ultimately lead to the death of the other.

———

To walk home to her village from the township where she attended middle school, June had to walk for two hours to the end of the concrete road that stopped another three hours' walk short of the village. Then, she had to walk through a rocky path that followed the curves of the mountainside, a path cut into a cliff edge that fell away to the vast panorama of the green valley below.

June's sister May and their cousin had helped open the path themselves. In the early 2000s, when May was ten years old and June was five, the village committee had organised all the families to carve a dirt path to the nearby road that was wide enough for a horse-drawn cart to pass through.

Every household was given a work quota to fulfil, but because June's and her cousin's parents were working in faraway cities at the time, their eldest daughters went to do the work for them, as Mulan-esque substitute conscripts. The adults heaved pickaxes to break the path into the mountainside; May and her cousin carted away wheelbarrows filled with rocks.

Some years later, the village paid more skilled workers to widen the road with explosives, leaving behind bed-sized roadside boulders that sometimes fell back down onto the path. The product of all their labours remained inaccessible to cars, but was still a significant improvement on the narrow trail that had existed before, which one had to tread slowly and carefully.

Now, June walked that path every weekend. When school finished on Friday, she would start walking at 5 p.m. and get home near midnight, the darkness slowing her steps. If she was desperate, she would spend Rmb5 – two weeks' living fees at the school – on a bus ticket from the township to the end of the concrete road, saving two hours' walking.

On the way back to school on Sunday afternoons, June carried in her backpack the bag of rice she ate during the week. Each student brought rice harvested from their own parents' paddies to the school kitchen to be steamed. June wondered why some children's rice was pearly white, whereas hers had pieces of yellow-brown husk; she concluded that the hand-driven rice-hulling machine that the families of her village shared was probably not as good as the ones the other villages had.

In addition to the rice, June's sister May liked to carry a jar of chilli oil in her backpack. The school served boiled vegetables for free as part of the government's poverty-alleviation programme. Still, to the sisters' tastes, the cooking lacked the salt, oil and spice that made a real meal. In adulthood,

June would joke that her childhood diet had given her a carnivorous appetite.

Rice was the mainstay of June's village, which was ringed with the stepped paddy fields common to China's mountainous south. Not having enough rice to eat was seen as a calamity, although sometimes it did happen. At such times, June's family would buy wheat noodles instead – in their eyes a poor substitute. In the village primary school, whenever it rained, the teacher would excuse himself from class to run home and gather water for his paddy.

————

June's idea of school, based on her experience at the village primary school, was that it was the place where she and her other friends got together to play all sorts of games of their own invention under the vaguest supervision from the teacher, who was meant to keep an eye on thirty children across six different grades simultaneously.

June's primary school had two teachers: one for the morning shift and one for the afternoon. The classroom had two blackboards facing each other on opposite walls; the younger three years of students would sit facing one side, and the older ones would sit facing the other. The teacher would walk from one end of the classroom to the other, giving a class to each side of students in turn. The school eventually put in a partition between the two groups to make it less distracting, but they still sat three years in one group, never getting the individual attention of the teacher.

Not that age groups mattered much to anyone. June had started school two years early, at the age of four. Her parents needed to put her in childcare, but there was no kindergarten in the village, so they persuaded the school to let her sit the first year of primary school three times. On one of June's first days of school, the group that she was part of, which included kids twice her age, was told to memorise a song from their textbook – a typical Chinese class exercise.

June was bewildered. She hadn't yet learned to read, and found it difficult to memorise the lines. The song was something about Beijing and Tiananmen Square, two places that didn't mean anything to her. Her teacher saw her stumbling over the words. 'If you can't focus, you'll have to stay behind after school!' he threatened. Eventually, he told her to stand by the blackboard at the front of the classroom, facing all the other students, and kept her there long after everyone else was dismissed. June felt humiliated, as well as hungry, since it was almost time for dinner. Only when her grandma came to the school to look for her did she manage to leave.

Apart from that bad start, June's memories of primary school were of having lots of fun. In their lunch breaks, the kids would run out into the mountainside and play house with the abundant materials they had to hand: a stick would be a person, a pile of dirt would be a kitchen. In the winters, when temperatures would drop to below freezing, each kid brought a metal pot of lit coal to put under their table to keep warm. In their lunch break, when the coal had burnt down to embers, they would head up the mountainside with their teachers to fetch firewood to top up their coal pots. The kids who knew how to wield axes would use them, while the others would break brittle branches against their shins.

Before the start of class when the kids lined up outside the wooden hut of their school, there were other games. One morning, some of the kids decided they would climb into the school through the windows, which were made of wooden planks with a gap between the planks for the light to filter in. They could just about fit through the gap; it felt like breaking a delicious taboo to be in the classroom before the teacher arrived.

June's grandma was illiterate, as was her father. But though they had no books of their own at home, June soon developed a love of reading. May's local township middle school had its own library, and she would bring home a different book for June every weekend.

June became the best student among the five in her year at primary school, with a score of 61 per cent in the final exams. Like most Chinese mothers, June's never praised her to her face. She displayed her pride in June in her own way. On the occasions she was home from her distant factory jobs, she would stick June's orange-and-gold school certificates straight onto their front door, so that everyone in the village could see.

But when June started going to the county town's middle school, she realised that her relative success didn't mean much in absolute terms, and in fact there were many gaps in her primary schooling.

She was expected to know the English alphabet but didn't. She didn't know in what order to write the brushstrokes of a Chinese character; to this day, she has trouble remembering. All these linguistic tools are acquired through repetition over a long period of time, and June felt she had missed her chance. In maths, she felt, it was easier to bridge the gaps: you could learn the techniques and master them more quickly than you could learn to write two thousand characters the right way. June started warming to maths and the sciences, although she loved literature.

The township middle school served the children of the rural areas around it and, as in all rural schools, everyone boarded during the week. This was a matter of convenience, as it was too far for many of them to walk every day, but also a matter of discipline. The teachers thought they would be better at raising the kids than their parents, who had generally not finished school themselves; the parents often agreed.

June's was a village of left-behind children brought up by themselves. Their grandparents could only 'keep them full and keep them warm', as the idiom went, and struggled to offer them support beyond that. Two of June's five primary-school classmates had already dropped out by the time June left for middle school. They either hung around their own farms or went to work in China's manufacturing provinces, Guangdong and Zhejiang, on the southern and eastern coasts. Although they were underage, employers wanted cheap and nimble hands on their assembly lines.

Truancy was a big problem. China's nine-year compulsory education system was passed into law in 1986, but had proven difficult to implement nationwide. In the late 1990s, when June was born, the Ministry of Education renewed its efforts to educate the countryside. Rural schools received additional funding from the larger, county-level governments, whereas before they had relied on donations from parents and funding from local townships, meaning the poorest areas inevitably had the poorest schools. But even with funds pooled across a larger region, it wasn't enough: poor counties continued to have the worst schools.

The Ministry of Education pressured rural teachers to retain students despite the fact that their environments were not conducive to schooling. Schools would be punished if their students dropped out before the end of middle school. Middle-school teachers had it worst: some of their twelve-year-olds arrived from primary school poorly equipped for the middle-school curriculum, and once they had fallen behind, there was very little the teachers felt they could do to get them back on track. In order to meet their targets, some teachers resorted to bribing the kids who had dropped out to attend classes when inspectors came round.

None of June's primary-school classmates made it into high school. Neither did May, who left the village at the age of fifteen with their aunt, who had recruited a few village girls to work in a garment factory near Shanghai, two days' travel away on China's eastern coast.

————

June's first impression of factory work was that it had made her sister beautiful beyond her wildest imaginings. June had still been at primary school when her sister left to work at the garment factory. The following Spring Festival, when May returned home for the first time, she arrived wearing new clothes.

The sisters had grown up wearing hand-me-downs and baggy sweatpants; now May was dressed sleekly all in black, wearing flesh-coloured stockings underneath a pair of black thigh-high leather boots. At that point, June didn't know the word for boots; even in winter, the village kids all wore cotton plimsolls.

Every spring, May would return home in a new outfit that reflected the styles of a city far beyond June's world. Working in Zhejiang, then the world's garment manufacturing capital, May could get her hands on fashions that June had only ever seen on TV.

May started straightening her hair and going to hairdressers for the first time, adopting a low-cut fringe that emphasised her large, thickly lashed eyes. She dyed her hair with a dark red tinge, as was the fashion among the girls in her factory at the time. She bought make-up. May had already been considered a village beauty in her early teens before she left for the city, and was now growing into her adult self.

May earned up to Rmb3,000 per month at her garment factory, a small fortune by rural standards, and sometimes splashed out on Rmb300 clothes for their mother. Her new-found spending power gave their mother something to brag to the neighbours about: 'I had my hair done at the salon in town today. I didn't mean to go, I'd never spend that much money on myself, but my eldest daughter tricked me. She told me she was going for herself and took me with her. Turns out she had already paid for me!'

Going out to work in a factory must be a splendid life, June concluded. You got to see the outside world, to live in a city, to earn money. She couldn't wait to follow in May's footsteps.

June felt lucky to have a sister. But in the countryside, it would have been easier for her family if she had had brothers instead. The preference for boys was strong. When arguments in the village turned nasty, neighbours would always reach for the same final rebuke against June's family: 'Your home only has daughters in it, while we have sons.' As the elder sister, May knew from a young age that she needed to be fierce in arguments to demonstrate that their family couldn't be bullied.

After their mother's sudden death, May and June relied on each other more than ever. It became clear to both girls, who were then thirteen and eighteen, that they would be responsible for supporting their father and grandma financially.

———

In the autumn, a few months after June moved back home in the wake of her mother's death, a stranger arrived in the village. The kids were told by their primary-school teachers that the newcomer, a recent retiree named Ms Song, was a volunteer teacher from Beijing.

Ms Song was not in fact from Beijing but from a city over a thousand miles away at the opposite, southern end of China. But to June and her teachers, China's big cities were essentially all the same: far away.

Ms Song had arrived in June's village as the result of a geographical error. She was unusual for her 1950s generation because she had been born in a city, and she hadn't intended to leave it for her post-retirement adventures.

Being the kind of woman who was unsatisfied unless she had a project to tackle, Ms Song had filled in a form to volunteer as a primary-school teacher with a charity that served schools across China. On the drop-down form, she selected her home city of high-rises and pedestrian overpasses whose railings were covered with bougainvillea that hung down, like magenta drapes, over six-lane expressways. Instead, she found herself assigned to one of China's poorest provinces, to a village three hours' walk away from the nearest concrete road. She realised she had made a mistake on the form, but took the post anyway out of curiosity.

June wanted to know what a person from Beijing looked like. She knew Ms Song was staying in the teachers' dormitory, on the second floor of the village primary school. One weekend, she and her best friend crept up to the school and yelled Ms Song's name. Then they lost their nerve and ran to hide round the corner of a neighbouring building.

'Who's there?' said Ms Song, coming out onto the first-floor balcony. She looked around, and saw two girls peering at her. They came closer. Ms Song walked down to greet them.

'Your hair is so beautiful,' June said, seeing curls permed by a professional hairdresser for the first time. In the village, experiments with perming started by heating metal chopsticks in the kitchen fire and often ended with the unmistakable smell of burning hair. June's hair was only just starting to grow out of the buzz cut that her sister had given both of them throughout her primary-school days. There wasn't enough time, shampoo or water to take care of anything else. But June had yearned for long hair and a mother who would plait it for her.

'Thank you,' Ms Song said. This was the first time June realised that it was polite to say 'thank you' in response to a compliment.

Ms Song asked where they lived and how old they were, and then she introduced herself.

'You don't look like you're fifty-five at all,' June marvelled. Ms Song had clear, light skin, and hadn't spent a day working under the searing mountain sun.

'Thank you,' Ms Song said again. In that moment, June knew she wanted to be like Ms Song when she was fifty-five.

After that, every weekend June would haggle with her grandma to let her visit Ms Song after she'd finished the farm work. Together they climbed the nearby mountains, whose peaks formed a jagged skyline. June took Ms Song on long hikes to find the deep caves under the mountains. She always respectfully called her Song *laoshi*: Teacher Song.

She was amazed that Teacher Song had so much time to do what she liked. There was no concept of retirement in the village: June's grandma, like all the other elderly, continued labouring in the fields until she couldn't physically work any more.

June loved Teacher Song's childlike qualities, which were somehow more apparent than those of her own peers, the children prematurely aged by chores and responsibility. She had never known someone who loved to wander so much, and who was so captivated by the ordinary beauty of the landscape. Teacher Song, June thought, was someone who really loved the world around her, someone who would pick the ignored orange wild flowers on the edges of the rice fields and arrange them into drinking-glass bouquets on the balconies of the primary school. *How lovely*, June thought, *how refreshing; how much she relishes and appreciates life!*

Apart from her short-lived rebellious phase in the county town, June's home life had been structured around work. In the autumn, they scraped dried sweetcorn off the cob to grind into cornmeal, and processed seemingly endless sacks of the harvested cobs before they were allowed to go to bed. At weekends, they scrambled up the mountainside in their plimsolls to pick herbal roots to sell.

Teacher Song injected playfulness back into June's life. She put together the village's first ever Children's Day, organising races and games on the road to the village. At primary school, June's teacher would mark the annual national holiday by saying, 'It's Children's Day tomorrow, you get the day off school, go home and help your grandparents in the fields.'

In the months since her mother had died, before meeting Teacher Song, June had been crying herself to sleep most nights. She felt the centre of her life had been torn away. Although she shared her time with her paternal grandma, she didn't share her deep unhappiness. They didn't have the words between them to describe what June was feeling.

But the third time they met, Teacher Song asked after June's health. She placed three fingers along June's wrist, feeling her pulse in the method of traditional Chinese medicine, and told her that her periods were irregular.

One weekend morning, as autumn became winter, June took Teacher Song for a hike towards a thermal spring half a day's walk away. It flowed in the shadows of a deep cave. Inside, one could sit in darkness on the rocky floor of the cave and watch the steam rise up the steep black walls, the droplets catching the faint light from far above. Teacher Song and June sat for a while, feeling the unfamiliar heat. On long walks like this, June would tell Teacher Song everything that was on her mind, things that she had never shared with anyone else before.

'Why can other girls hold hands with their mothers? Why is my life so unfair?' June said.

'Life isn't about fairness or unfairness,' Teacher Song replied gently. 'You will grow from this too. You will have many more good things come to you. What you can do now is prepare for those good opportunities.'

———

Under Teacher Song's guidance, June resolved to commit herself to her studies. She wanted to see the outside world that Teacher Song described, and to experience the opportunities that Teacher Song persuaded her lay further down the road away from the village.

Her grandma, who had worked on the farm her entire life, thought that there was no point in studying hard. Her advice to June was to learn just enough to be able to write and read her own name, car number plates and bus timetables. In the end, like all the other kids in the village, she assumed June would go to work on a farm or in a factory. After June graduated from middle school, at the age of fifteen, her grandma planned to buy her a pig to raise. Extra studying was simply excess work.

What's more, if you were a girl, investing in your education was doubly pointless from your family's point of view: you would be married off to work for another family. June's grandma did not love her or her sister any less for being girls; she simply accepted the Chinese proverb that daughters are 'water poured onto a neighbour's garden'.

June's grandma told June, 'If you're good at it, then go to school. If you're not, then work on the farm with me.'

'I'll go to school whether I'm good at it or not,' June answered.

Despite the beautiful impression she had initially had of her sister's life at the garment factory, after her mother's death June had started to resent the idea of ending up on an assembly line. By the early 2010s, all the older kids in June's village had left school for full-time work. She had the persistent feeling that, if she didn't find a way out through studying, she would have to resign herself to the same fate.

June realised that the outside world was much bigger than even her sister had known. In her middle-school library, June devoured the memoirs and travelogues of Sanmao, a writer beloved by Chinese teens. Sanmao was born in south-western China in the 1940s and rejected the traditional path prescribed to the women of her era. She travelled the world, living in Taiwan, Germany, Spain, the Canary Islands, Central America and the Sahara Desert. Sanmao wrote about her itinerant life in a carefree style, as if anyone could simply pack their bags, leave home, and teach themselves to drive on sandy desert tracks. June particularly loved her book *The Stories of the Sahara* and wanted to see the expansive desert for herself.

Sanmao had also been a teenage misfit with a great love of music and literature, and had dropped out of school after being bullied by her teacher. In a song called 'Off Track', she wrote:

A timid kid was scared of her teacher
So scared she became a little soldier, deserting her post
locking herself into walls of books . . .
In the days off track
There are no years, no months, no Children's Day
little hands
hard as they try, couldn't open
the deadlock of being marked a bad child.

June had left behind in the county town her bad-child days, as well as the teachers who had looked down on her. She made a fresh start at the township middle school.

When the orange-and-gold certificates started reappearing in June's house, she pinned them up on the wall inside the entrance herself. She decided she wanted to do what she had seen few do before her: at the age of fifteen, instead of raising the pig her grandma had promised her, she wanted to pass the entrance exams for high school.

3

Women's work
Leiya

When Leiya was a small girl, she started to fear becoming a woman. The women of her village laboured in the fields and laboured in the home. They toiled on weekdays, weekends and even more so on holidays, when they prepared the feasts. Women worked themselves to the bone during Spring Festival, the happiest week of the year.

But by far the worst part, Leiya thought, was having to give birth to sons. She watched the women of the village going through endless cycles of swelling bellies. Conceiving, aborting, birthing. For however long it took for a son to come along. Giving birth without a thought for your own life. An inevitable life. In Leiya's words: a shit life.

Leiya did not want this life. At the same time, she couldn't think of what other life there might be. The informal rules of the village were laid out very clearly: families without sons got bullied. Her maternal grandparents, who she lived with as a small child, received earfuls of this. 'So-and-so's got four sons, but look at you with your three daughters.'

She loved her grandparents, and hated to hear them attacked in this way. It could be for the smallest perceived slight, like a drip of wastewater on someone else's vegetable patch. Sometimes she wondered if her neighbours looked for opportunities to pick fights. The only way she might avoid the same fate, she knew, was by being luckier in the endless cycle: having a son. Otherwise, it was conceiving, aborting, birthing.

Or she could leave. In the late 1980s, soon after Leiya was born, her parents had gone out to work in the factory towns springing up in the Pearl River Delta on China's southern coast. Her grandparents gave her shelter, but they had their own fields to rake, and not enough of anything to give Leiya or her little brother. Towards the end of primary school, her parents took her back to their old home, away from her grandparents. But when Leiya started middle school, at the age of twelve, they left again to earn money to pay for her and her brother's school fees. By then, she was old enough to cook for both of them.

In her early teens, Leiya became tall and lanky, her trousers too short for her legs, leaving an embarrassing stretch of calf exposed to the winter air. Every weekend, she and her brother walked an hour home from the nearest school in the county town, where they boarded during the week. When they got home, there was nobody waiting for them. Nobody to heat the water in the winter for their weekly bath, nobody to do their laundry. Not enough to wear. Leiya often walked back to school in damp clothes that clung to her, chilling her. Secretly she longed to be clean, to be warm, even to be beautiful. She remembered the look her father gave her once on one of his visits home: a sorrowful glance, pitying his dirty child. Then, a few days later, he was gone again.

Other parents came to the school with additional food for her classmates. But Leiya always felt hungry. One morning in the first term of her third year of middle school, after several days of barely eating anything, Leiya woke in her dormitory with a sore throat and no energy in her limbs. She couldn't face climbing the three flights of stairs to the classroom, so she gave up on class and went back to sleep.

She was fifteen at the time. That winter holiday, she left school for good. For Chinese New Year, her parents had decided to bring her and her brother to Shenzhen, the city where they were working. She was beyond excited to see the city for the first time, and kept her eyes open the entire day and half the night of the bus journey, gazing at the novel lights of the cities they passed through. This was where her parents lived their real lives, among millions of strangers.

After they arrived in Shenzhen, Leiya's brother became severely ill, and her parents kept him there so they could take care of him. At the end of the Chinese New Year holiday, Leiya was faced with going back to the village alone.

So she didn't. It wasn't that she didn't want to go to school. She just didn't want to go back home. There was nothing waiting for her in her dormitory, in the empty house in the village. When her teachers rang to ask why she had missed the start of term, she was silent.

———

Leiya spent a couple of months hanging around at her parents' and helping to care for her brother, who eventually recovered, and then she started looking for work. She'd been sleeping on a bunk bed that belonged to one of the men they shared the flat with, and once he came back from the Chinese New Year holiday, she had nowhere to sleep. She needed to find a job that would provide her with a dormitory bed.

Leiya was underage. But that was easily solved back then: Rmb50, a few days' wages, got her a fake identity certificate. It was made by one of the many agents who graffitied their adverts onto the walls of the city's factory district. The certificate was a little booklet stuck together with glue, bearing a fake identity number that Leiya had thought up herself by looking at her parents' identity numbers. The certificate said she was three years older than she really was.

Leiya hadn't finished her compulsory schooling, but on the application forms she ticked all the boxes saying otherwise. It was 2001, the year of China's entry to the World Trade Organization. China's cheap labour was available to the world, and foreign investors were setting up factories in the Pearl River Delta. Migrants from the countryside followed, many looking as young as Leiya.

Leiya landed an interview with a garment factory. When she arrived, she felt the hiring manager's eyes sweep over her dismissively.

'What year of school are you in?' he asked.

'I've finished school,' she said.

'Show me your graduation certificate then,' he said. Something in his voice, as if he had seen a hundred versions of her, made Leiya think: what a rude man. And that led her to say:

'It's not like this is the kind of place that needs graduates, is it? I've left the certificate at home; I'll bring it tomorrow.'

He signed her up for a shift, and by the time she arrived the next morning, the matter of the graduation certificate had been forgotten. She put together gift boxes for the factory's children's clothing line, earning Rmb600 ($70) a month, working from 8 a.m. to 2 a.m. As a fifteen-year-old in the city, Leiya was already earning three times what the average farmer earned back home.

But box-packing was a simple task, and soon Leiya wanted to learn some technical skills. After an introduction from a family friend, she moved to another garment factory, and started learning to use the industrial sewing machines. She didn't like the line managers there: they ruled by yelling, throwing unfinished clothes at the workers, and telling them they were stupid. She left after three months.

After that, Leiya didn't find work for half a year. In the early 2000s, young rural migrants were pouring into the Pearl River Delta. They would queue up for a whole day whenever a factory was looking for staff, and hiring managers took bribes to bump people up the list. Some factories only hired in the evenings to avoid dealing with the huge crowds of applicants during the day.

For that half-year, Leiya was homeless. That was the worst part of leaving a factory: no job meant no dormitory bed. There was an extensive network of people who had migrated to the city from Leiya's province, and this gave her a community to fall back on, a night or two at each auntie's flat, taking someone's husband's bed while he was out for the night shift. There had been a space in the corridor of her parents' flat, where she'd pull a wooden board over the cold tiles to sleep on, but it was mostly occupied by her brother these days. Every time Leiya found some nook in which to spend the night, she hated the feeling of dirt on her skin. She had just started getting her periods. She longed for hot showers. She wanted to be clean.

She took it as a miracle when she finally found a job at a leatherwear factory. The job paid around Rmb1,000 per month, depending on how many pieces she made. The staff wore coloured uniforms to signal their place in the factory hierarchy: blue for assembly-line workers, yellow for assembly-line managers, white for the senior managers.

Although the factory was owned by a Taiwanese boss, her colleagues were all Sichuanese girls around her age. They worked over sixteen hours a day in the heat of the factory floor, shouting to make themselves heard over the continuous rattle of the sewing machines. They stitched together the leather phone-holders that fashionable businessmen used to wear clipped to their belts to hold their Nokias. When the women got a particularly tough piece of leather to stitch, they would curse in the Sichuanese dialect, and Leiya started copying them. She got on well with her dorm-mates, and even with her assembly-line manager, who liked Leiya for her rashness. Leiya sometimes made mistakes, but she worked very quickly – the most important quality for an assembly-line worker. Whenever they could find some time in their long days, the assembly-line manager would invite Leiya and some of her fellow workers to her place for a spicy Sichuanese meal.

She spent two years there, but she wasn't happy. What bothered her most about the factory wasn't the strenuous work – it was the way that the factory managers took every opportunity to squeeze the workers. In the bathrooms, a female manager stood by the shower stalls chiding them to hurry up, to save on hot-water costs. They had no hot water to drink, or to wash their clothes in. Every minute of the day was taken up by working, eating rapidly, queuing for the showers, or doing laundry. There was barely any time after the evening shift to wash: overtime could stretch until 1 or 2 a.m. The next day, everything would start again at 7 a.m. Leiya knew that going from the dormitory to the warehouse every day, seven days a week, was not what she wanted.

The factory floor was entirely female, but every now and then the male boss appeared, and he liked to line up some of the workers in a row and ask them, one by one, if they had a boyfriend yet. Leiya hated him. She could see his intentions a mile off. But no matter how much she resented the factory, she didn't dare quit. She feared becoming homeless again.

Instead, she became as rebellious as she could without getting fired. She started to miss shifts and spend her mornings wandering outside in the city. She convinced some of her dorm-mates to join her. Together, they'd leave the dorms at 6.30 a.m. By the time the managers came to the dorms to chase people up at 7 a.m., they were gone. They wandered aimlessly around the city, with nothing to spend or do. They looked at the sky, rode the ferries back and forth across the lake, having dumb fun. They looked for work in other factories.

After about half a month of this, one of the factory managers told Leiya she had stacked up enough fines for her no-shows not to receive any salary at all that month. 'Your colleagues are working hard overtime,' he said, trying to guilt-trip her.

Leiya shrugged it off. She had turned eighteen that year, and her few weeks of sauntering around the city had given her some swagger. 'Why should I come to work if I won't get paid?' she fired back. The factory wanted to keep her, and offered Leiya a promotion, which would mean she could trade her blue uniform in for the higher-status yellow, but Leiya was set on leaving. She gathered the other six girls in her dormitory, and they resigned together.

4

The school on the outskirts
Siyue

At the start of Siyue's third and final year of high school, her parents came back from the city of Shenzhen, and moved into a flat near Siyue's small-town high school. That way, her mother Sulan could help cook for her while she prepared for the university entrance exams, known as *gaokao*.

Siyue had been trying to make up for the two years of classroom rote-learning that had washed over her by teaching herself using her own methods. But the *gaokao* rewarded memorisation, so she needed to cram like all the others, even though it didn't come naturally to her.

School began at 7.30 a.m. and finished at 9 p.m. Then Siyue and her classmates stayed up beyond midnight, filling in multiple-choice exam papers. It was the only way of studying they knew. Siyue went to school six days a week, and had around six hours of sleep each night. It was never enough sleep. Seeing how hard she was working, her mother chided her less.

When Siyue's mother Sulan had been in high school, she had had much less homework; her school day would end at 5 p.m., and teachers couldn't assign more work because they knew their students had farm chores to finish. When Sulan got home, she would stay up until midnight threshing barley by hand. She would tie the stalks into heavy bundles, then sling each bundle over her shoulder and down against the millstone, over and over again, until her arms ached.

Now Sulan saw her daughter's mental, not physical, labours, and she began to sympathise with her. Siyue was old enough to take care of her own studies, Sulan thought; all she needed to do was support her. She asked Siyue's teachers to simply encourage her, no matter what grades she got.

———

Just before Siyue's birthday in 2001, the prices of shares on the Shanghai Stock Exchange reached an all-time high. Then, the bubble burst. The market went into a deep slump for the next year, losing almost a third of its value.

Because of Siyue's father's financial speculation, nearly all of her parents' savings were trapped in stocks. Over the years that followed, the family depended on the week-to-week whims of stock movements to determine how much cash they could withdraw for groceries.

Siyue would often overhear her parents discussing their financial problems. Her father's anger at his bad luck permeated their flat. He would stay up late into the night, reading about stocks, and then snap at her for making a noise when she got up for school at 5.30 a.m. She and her mother could sense his moods, could feel his clenched teeth; they could read the smallest gestures that signalled an impending storm. She tried to spend as little time at home as possible, hanging out at friends' houses.

Her father had previously taken charge of Siyue's education by forcing her to study sciences rather than humanities in high school. That meant that in addition to the core subjects of maths, Chinese and English, the majority of Siyue's *gaokao* marks came from physics, chemistry and biology. Siyue had always preferred the humanities, but her father held the popular opinion that the country needed more scientists, and that studying science would help her get a job.

In her third year of high school, Siyue started watching a popular TV show called *Outlook*. It was an experiment by the state broadcaster, Central China Television, in putting on a more light-hearted show aimed at a young audience. Its goal was to improve viewers' cross-cultural understanding, and featured teenagers speaking English and Chinese in everyday contexts, simply having fun.

Siyue was drawn to the scenes of girls not much older than her effortlessly travelling around the world and casually striking up conversations with strangers. She felt intense envy. She wanted a life like that, but she didn't know where she might find it.

She had once harboured middle-school dreams of becoming a radio anchor; she had always been a talkative child. Back in her Shenzhen school, she had hosted school radio shows, and volunteered to MC during school performances – she liked being onstage. But when she told her mother about these dreams, Sulan had snapped that real broadcasters-in-training would have started taking private classes years ago, and she had no chance.

Without any other career plan, and at her father's insistence, Siyue applied to study biology at university. Her exam season started inauspiciously on the sports field, with the physical education assessment. She almost didn't make it to the end of the 800-metre race; her best friend pulled her across the finish line.

When Siyue's university entrance scores came back, they were neither great nor terrible. Her poor science scores had been buoyed a little by her good English and Chinese scores, but the overall result was mediocre. And mediocre scores meant disappointment in her home province of Jiangsu, one of China's most populous, where as a result the competition for university quotas is most intense.

That summer, Siyue started what she thought would be a huge argument with her father. She told him she would never let him dictate her life for her again. She was going to study English.

Her father didn't put up much of a fight. He had other battles to deal with. That same summer, Siyue's mother Sulan discovered the extent of his stock losses, which he had been trying to hide. When he kept refusing Sulan access to the family bank account, she marched over to the exchange where he did his trading, and logged into his account. She discovered there was only Rmb30,000 left: 3 per cent of the 1 million they had initially invested.

By the time she decided to rebel against her father, it was too late for Siyue to reapply for English programmes through the public university system. Siyue found an advert for a private college teaching English in Beijing. Despite their financial problems, her parents were willing to put up the tuition, at Rmb10,000 a year, thinking it was Siyue's last chance to study. The advert boasted of hosting teachers from Beijing's top foreign-language universities. Siyue didn't know how the private education system worked or how it compared with the state system of degree qualifications – she just wanted a place to learn.

When she arrived, she found a school far on the outskirts of Beijing, surrounded by fields. It was still in the process of building built, and the floors were filled with uncovered potholes. There were very few teachers to speak of. It was so empty that it felt like a practical joke. She soon realised the headmaster was a scam artist.

Though Siyue had nothing but disgust for the headmaster, she was amazed by how kind her new dorm-mates were. Unlike the girls in her secondary schools in Shenzhen and her home town, all of these women came from different parts of China, and there was no single dominant gang. Everyone was making friends afresh.

Siyue shared a dorm with five other girls. In the hallway stood six lockers, stacked in pairs. Inside, bunk beds were pressed against three of the walls, with a window on the fourth wall, beneath which was a small table. Siyue and her dorm-mates lived in tight company and got on well.

To their parents and high-school teachers, Siyue's five dorm-mates were the 'bad kids': they were at the private college because they had done poorly at the *gaokao* exams. Their parents, mostly small-business owners, had enough savings to pay for a few more years of education.

To Siyue, her dorm-mates were the most human people she had ever met. They had personalities, opinions, senses of humour. They were down to earth, warm and curious about one another. They were the opposite of the 'good kids' at Siyue's high school, who were disciplined, cold and hypercompetitive. Original thoughts would distract you from your studies, so the 'good kids' had to give up their personalities. Perhaps, Siyue thought, her new 'bad girl' friends had kept their colourful personalities by being resigned to not doing well at school.

The good kids had ignored Siyue: they weren't interested in anyone who they felt was irrelevant to their exam scores. But one night soon after the start of the college term, when Siyue was lying in her dorm bed feeling nauseous and feverish, the girl in the bunk below noticed her heavy breathing. She wordlessly got up, poured out a glass from the room's hot-water flask, and raised it to her top bunk. Siyue drank it and fell back to sleep. She felt safe with her sisters in their cosy dorm. They became her first group of close girlfriends.

Siyue's dorm-mates each had their own reasons for coming to college, most of which weren't to do with studying. One had been accepted into a proper university but had given up her place to be closer to her boyfriend. The girl on the bunk below her wasn't into studying at all, but very into meeting boys.

Throughout her teens Siyue had wanted so badly to start dating. Apart from her grandfather, there had been no male role models she'd felt close to during her childhood. She was acutely aware of this lack, and she knew she wanted male affection. She was a dreamer who loved a Jane Austen ending. But she didn't think she was attractive enough to deserve one.

Siyue had a slim, heart-shaped face framed by softly wavy hair, a broad smile, wide almond-shaped eyes, and a slim nose with a high nose bridge — a feature valued by Chinese beauty standards. But with typically East Asian single eyelids, rather than the rarer and more desired creased eyelid, she sometimes wondered if she had the kind of face that would never make a Chinese man look twice.

———

When Jiaolong first started sitting close to Siyue at lectures and hanging around her in the breaks between classes, she assumed he was interested in her dorm-mate Jinghua, who worked part-time as a model. Siyue and Jinghua went everywhere together, and Siyue assumed it was natural that

Jiaolong, the funniest, most confident boy in their class, had a crush on Jinghua.

But Jiaolong kept turning up, even when Jinghua wasn't there. After a while, Siyue started to think again.

Jiaolong was four years older than Siyue: a big gap for an eighteen-year-old girl. After high school he had gone into the army, then opened a bar for a year, before enrolling in the private college. Unlike Siyue, he wasn't set on graduating: he was studying for the sake of studying. But he encouraged Siyue's dedication to her studies, and many of their dates were spent studying together.

Siyue loved how protective he was. She liked having him with her when she walked home at night, along the unlit road from the bus stop, in the middle of the fields where the college stood.

It was possibly the most virtuous romance one could have had in the eyes of traditional Chinese parents, but Siyue of course didn't tell them. On the nights when she stayed over with Jiaolong, if her parents called the fixed-line phone in her dorm, her dorm-mates would handle the situation. They'd pick up, since letting it ring out would have also been suspicious, and mumble, 'Oh, what's that? Can't hear a thing. The line must be bad.' For the first time in her life, Siyue felt she had a family fully on her side.

5

One hundred nights of struggle
June

When June was in her teens, Teacher Song would return to June's village every year for a few weeks at a time. She particularly liked to come in the springtime, when the mountainside was carpeted with wild alpine flowers. She also tried to bring others with her from the world beyond the mountains. One year, she came back for Children's Day with a master's student from Chongqing University. June didn't know what a master's degree was, so she went to ask the newcomer.

That year, a distant cousin on June's grandma's side got into a first-class university. June didn't know what university entailed, but she did hear that the cousin's family held a banquet for him, complete with expensive *baijiu*, sorghum liquor. University students in their area were rare, and deserved a grand celebration; June felt that meant it must be worth trying for. She also had the impression that going to university meant having lots of time to read books, which she had always enjoyed. And, of course, Teacher Song kept on telling her that university would expand her horizons. June started to form hopes of not only getting into high school, but also university.

She shared these hopes with a friend in the village who had dropped out at the end of primary school and wanted to know why June was studying so hard.

'I want to go to university,' she told him.

He found it ridiculous, and laughed. 'Go on then, I'll give you Rmb10,000 if you get in.'

June learned to keep her dreams to herself. As a fourteen-year-old, university seemed so distant. Yet June had also learned that time was a silvery thing that could quickly evaporate. The two years since her mother's death and her return to the village from the county town had felt like no time at all, yet she also felt she had lived infinite lives. After she was given a notebook as a prize in a school essay competition, June started to mark the passage of time with diary entries.

If you were still here

If you were still here, I'd smile back at the smiling face of the clouds,
and I would smile even more splendidly, the kind of smile
that you can't stop smiling.

Looking at the towering mountains,
no matter what thunderstorms may dance on them,
they will stay standing tall.

If you were here,
I'm sure you'd teach me how to be strong like them
I'm sure you'd teach how to rise to the occasion
I'm sure you'd teach me how to face what I don't understand

In the dawn light, the waves strike against the shore,

the waters seem so brave.
If you were here,
I'm sure you'd let me be like the waves,
brave like them, like them unafraid,
and even though the path I walk might have thunderstorms,
still surging forward, vigorously.
If you were here,

would I have a few less scars?
would I have a few more smiles?
would I hold my head higher?
would I walk with a firmer pace?

Watchfully waiting: it feels like I've been doing that since I was born. That spring, I sat in the field where the grass had started to grow long, watching you as you walked past with a basket of seeds and a basket of fertiliser. You'd sometimes turn your head to look at me and you'd smile, or praise me warmly with a few sentences . . .

Back then, I always wanted to grow up a little quicker, so I could spend all the seasons with you, but when I was a little older you'd started running all over the world, and I'd want to be even older still, so I'd be able to run around with you, and before I'd even thought of where we might go, my father walked through the door of our house with a jar of ashes, and you were nowhere. And when I'd grown up a little, you didn't come back.

———

I can't make sense of time. Some things I had thought of as very recent are further and further away; some I thought of as far are in fact slowly nearing. Like the zhongkao *exams [to enter high school], something I didn't even dare to think about when I was little, which are now coming into view.*

When the zhongkao *exams come, will I lose sleep the entire night before my exams? Will I be really nervous when I look at the test paper? Will I be as careless as I usually am when answering the questions? These kinds of scenes emerge over and over again in my head, my hidden fear revealing itself. It's not too early for me to think about this now, I still have time to prepare, right? I had thought that the last term of third grade would be a distant journey with an amazing view, but suddenly when I'm in the middle of it, I feel a little uncomfortable.*

In terms of going to high school, I think my hopes are tiny. When it comes to zhongkao, *will I see that there are too many students much better than me, and give up? Will I see someone else completely filling out their test paper and be too scared to start writing? Will I be sat in a dark corner, and feel dejected? Why am I so unconfident?*

———

At the end of her third year of middle school, when she was almost fifteen, June and her classmates travelled to the county town to take their high-school entrance exams, the *zhongkao* ('middle exams'). She would be competing against thousands of other kids who had grown up in the town, as well as those from other poor villages.

Ever since her mother's death had made her move back to the village, June only got to go to the county town twice a year, at the start of the autumn and spring terms, to buy new textbooks. There was no bookshop in the township where her middle school was based.

June and her classmates boarded a bus the school had organised; the two-hour journey felt like their first ever school outing. Most of June's classmates treated it as a holiday – they weren't going to get into high school, so they might as well have some fun in town. They felt like fish that had escaped from a tank into a wide lake. They had two days to 'settle in' before the exams started, which they spent visiting the various parks and attractions around the county town.

Their school had booked them accommodation in a hostel, with four students to a room. It was the end of the month of June, in the feverish week when more than 10 million schoolchildren across China took the *zhongkao*. The town was lower down in the mountains than the villages, and hotter. The kids had nothing to protect themselves from the sun, and June's hostel had no air conditioning or even electric fans. The heat combined with the stress of the three-day exams meant June spent the nights sleeplessly turning in her bunk bed.

Since she'd spent a year in the county town before, June became the guide for her classmates, taking them to the places she used to have fun. At the same time, she harboured a gnawing anxiety. She didn't think anyone expected her or her classmates to get into any high school, much less a good one. She felt badly prepared. She was very aware of all the gaps she had left in her learning.

When she got her scores back, June was shocked to find that she had gotten into the county-town high school. Her grades were good enough to have gotten her into an even better school in the nearest city, but nobody had told her beforehand to apply there. As expected, very few of her middle-school classmates passed.

———

At the age of fifteen, with no relatives or friends nearby, June rented a flat in the county town near her new high school. It was relatively cheap, because it was a single room, with a traditional stove on the floor and a bed. There was no refrigerator, so she bought her food from the market most days.

Every morning, June would get up around 6 a.m., buy a steamed bun from the street-food stall by the school gates, and eat it as she climbed the stairs to her classroom. The school lacked a canteen, so at noon she would go home to cook for herself.

She made simple meals since she had little energy left over from studying. Some months, she would make nothing but noodles boiled with some cabbage leaves and seasoning. Noodles were easy and quick, and giant heads of Chinese napa cabbage could keep for weeks without going off. But her stomach would hurt after too many days of this pattern.

Throughout June's three years of high school, she obsessively fantasised about two things: sleeping and eating. She longed to sleep in at the weekend, but she had Saturday classes, and by the last year of high school, Sunday classes too.

June looked forward to the few days every term when her sister May and her husband – who she had met on China's east coast while doing factory work – might pass through town, because they would bring her something nice to eat, or a red envelope of money, or even take her out for a meal.

On Sunday afternoons, which were sometimes the only spare time she had in the week, June would scrub her clothes by hand while resenting the time she had to waste doing so. She relieved her boredom by listening to podcasts on her smartphone. She particularly liked the speeches of Yu Minhong, the founder of New Oriental, the country's biggest private education company.

In 2013, around the time June started high school, a film had been released loosely based on Yu's life called *American Dreams in China*. Filled with slapstick comedy, it describes the lives of three young men from poor backgrounds who dream of studying in the US. The character based on Yu is repeatedly denied an entry visa, but the three end up founding an English-language tuition company together and striking it rich.

The film includes several dramatic shots of Yu's speeches, superimposed against a stadium of cheering fans: he is a rock star, easy and confident. By the time the film was released, Yu had become a dollar billionaire and was known in China as the godfather of English teaching.

A witty public speaker with a self-deprecating sense of humour, Yu liked to mix personal anecdotes with pep talks:

Hew a stone of hope out of a mountain of despair and you can make your life a splendid one.

In the beginning, there were no roads in the world; only as people began travelling did roads come into being. Successful roads are formed not when people roam aimlessly, but when they are headed in the same direction. The same is true for New Oriental; it was formed as people gathered to study.

———

June carried on being the top in her class, but she knew it wasn't that good a class. As the three years of high school passed by, university drew nearer. Far from being a dream, it was becoming inevitable. The only uncertainty was where she'd end up.

China has around 1,400 universities that grant undergraduate degrees. About a hundred of these belong to the 'Project 211' group of elite universities, where less than half a million students enter each year. The competition to squeeze into China's top universities is higher than almost anywhere else in the world. Overall, China's 211 group admit five out of every hundred students who apply, the same rate as Harvard University. Beijing's Peking University accepts just one in a hundred applicants.

Being from a family with a Beijing *hukou* helps tremendously, because universities have a quota for local students. In one year, Beijing's two top universities took 84 out of every 10,000 applicants from Beijing but fewer than 5 out of every 10,000 applicants from some of China's poorest provinces, including June's.

June aimed high for her top five choices. For number 6, her fall-back option, she chose a local university, one she was sure to get into.

Towards the end of high school, Teacher Song visited June in the county town where she was studying. Squeezed between June's classes and her evening study session, Teacher Song took June for dinner at a Western restaurant that had just opened. That invitation in itself – to eat Western food – sounded like a luxury to June, who had spent the previous week eating from street-food stalls.

Sitting in the restaurant, Teacher Song poured tea for June from a glass teapot filled with large flowers steeped in a light pink liquid. After they finished eating and got up to leave, June held on to Teacher Song tightly and cried, not knowing when they would see each other again after she finished school: whether she went to university or out to work, she would have to go far from her home town.

'I hope you live very well,' Teacher Song said.

———

In 2020, 44 million students were accepted to universities in China. Nationwide, that is over half of the 79 million who graduate from high school, and less than a third of the 140 million of the same cohort who finished middle school together.

None of June's middle-school classmates were admitted to university. But each of the five girls who were June's neighbours in her block of flats got in. June concluded that children move in groups: if one boy in a dormitory starts smoking, everyone else will follow; if one girl starts getting up early to study, everyone else will, too.

Just before June turned eighteen, she took her university entrance exams over the course of two days, along with the rest of the country. Two feverish days in summer are all it takes to fix one's future.

Universities publish their quotas for different provinces every summer. The quota system disadvantages larger provinces, and also leads to uncertainty for applicants: if, one year, more students in your province apply for a certain course, then you will have to score higher to get in.

Chinese universities admit in rounds. First, the departments of the first-tier universities go down the list of applicants, from the top *gaokao* score downwards, until they fill their quota of students. The lowest score they admit is called the 'score line', and this varies every year, depending on the number and quality of applicants and the provincial quota. Strategising about getting into one's preferred university involves second-guessing the choices of all your peers.

There is an industry for this: educational consultancies charge between a few thousand to tens of thousands of renminbi for advice on how to tactically craft the best university preference list. About a quarter of a million students use these, and the industry is growing rapidly. Consultants give advice such as telling students to gun for the most prestigious university they can by applying for the easiest degree course to get into.

But June had filled in her preferences without much thought or guidance other than her own ambition. She slipped down her list of universities one by one, rejected by all of her first five choices, until finally she met the requirements for her last choice: the safe local school.

Part Two

6

Surveying Shenzhen
Sam

It was the sweltering summer holiday of Sam's first year of university, and she was spending it walking across unfamiliar streets in her home city of Shenzhen, knocking on strangers' doors. She had lived here since she was a baby, only leaving for university, yet only now was she fully seeing it for the first time.

Sam had taken a summer job at her university's sociology department, collecting responses for a new research project: the first nationwide study of China's changing labour force.

By then, in the early 2010s, the researchers noted that after three decades of 'market-oriented practice', 'China's economy has entered a new stage'. The country's social structure was changing, and better data was needed to understand these changes.

Shenzhen was a young city, almost as young as Sam herself. It had been a collection of fishing villages before the boom began in the 1980s, when it became the experimental site for the Communist Party's tentative embrace of capitalism. Deng Xiaoping, the country's leader after Mao, brought in the Reform and Opening Up era in 1978 by allowing private businesses and markets to exist alongside the state-planned economy. He was trying to introduce a more pragmatic socialism – one that would modernise the country's industries and create prosperity.

Sam's parents were part of the fledgling urban middle class, having moved to Shenzhen from the surrounding Guangdong countryside for work. In the late 1980s, when Sam's mother Zhao was eighteen, officials from the local government labour bureau had gone to her village. They wanted young girls with nimble fingers. They promised her Rmb70 a month – as much as party cadres earned in her village, and much more than her father and grandpa earned. Zhao and a hundred others went with the recruiters to Shenzhen.

Chosen for its proximity to Hong Kong, Shenzhen housed China's first 'Special Economic Zone', an area separated from the rest of the country by barbed-wire fences, where foreign businesses could invest and build factories. Zhao sat on the assembly line of a Japanese-owned radio factory inside the zone. With the dozen other women on her line, she had to assemble each module within a minute; in an hour, the whole factory produced fifty to sixty radios. She had a goal in mind: to assemble them so quickly that she would be promoted enough times to receive a Shenzhen *hukou* from her company. If she succeeded, she would never have to go home to her village.

Three years in Shenzhen and some three hundred thousand radios later, Zhao got her *hukou*. She married Sam's father, a man from near her home town, who had also gone to Shenzhen to work as a government accountant.

By the late 1980s, the opening up of private markets had brought with it a rise in inequality that was unprecedented in the Communist era, as well as a higher cost of living for urban workers.

Along with calls for more government transparency, these frustrations brought students and residents of Beijing onto the streets in June 1989. The government, led by Deng Xiaoping, opened fire on the protesters in Tiananmen Square. Later that year, the party leadership watched the fall of the Berlin Wall that had separated its Communist and capitalist sides. Two years later came the dissolution of the Soviet Union, thus leaving China as the last remaining large state under Communist rule.

China's politicians saw all these as warning signs. More officials argued for central planning of the economy to rein in the inflation and chaos that they saw as the result of overly rapid growth. But Deng Xiaoping still wanted to make the argument for increased marketisation. In January 1992, after he had officially retired, Deng made secret plans for a 'Southern Tour' of China. On the tour, he urged his allies to accelerate reform. 'We'll definitely speed things up,' replied Shenzhen's number one. Historians now believe the Southern Tour cemented China's turn towards global trade.

Around that time, Zhao gave birth to Sam. Soon after, Sam's father was promoted in his job, and the government gave him a flat on the fourteenth floor of the first high-rise in the city to be built with a lift.

That was how Sam came to be born into a special sliver of her generation: the urban middle class, with a city *hukou*. She enjoyed small luxuries Zhao's mother had never seen in her village childhood. Their flat had a TV, another perk of her father's government job, which became Sam's preschool obsession.

As a toddler, Sam wanted to watch TV from the moment she woke up. Zhao had had an electricity-free childhood, and she sensed it was not going to be good for Sam to spend the entirety of hers glued to the screen. But she didn't know how to redirect her daughter's attention. She shared her concerns with a friend who worked as a teacher, and he gave her a piece of advice: take her to the library.

Shenzhen had started renovating and building its municipal libraries in the late 1980s, trying to create a civilised citizenry for their new city. At Sam's primary school, the teachers offered after-school workshops to the parents, stressing the importance of reading for their children's development.

When Sam was little, the Shenzhen Children's Library opened a half-hour walk from her home. It was ahead of its time: the first dedicated children's library in all of Guangdong, Hong Kong and Macau. In the context of rural China, where children are customarily comforted with food and warmth but not intellectual attention, a children's library was groundbreaking. It had a mission: 'When the children are wise, so is the nation; when the children are strong, so is the nation.'

Zhao persisted in taking Sam to the library every weekend and letting her loose, hoping something about the book-filled rooms would transform her daughter into the good student she herself had never been.

At first, Sam didn't know what she was meant to do. She initially gravitated towards the library's TV screens, which played educational shows that were not quite as absorbing as the scenes she saw on her home TV. After she grew bored of the screens, she discovered the picture books, and thus began her life of being buried in books.

———

When Sam was finishing primary school, her mother had an accidental pregnancy. Under the one-child policy, in some parts of China, doctors used to routinely insert an IUD, a copper coil that acts as a long-term contraceptive, into a woman's uterus after she had given birth to their first child.

Zhao had started getting pain from her IUD, and her doctor removed it for a few months so that her body could recover. During that window, Zhao got pregnant again, and decided to keep it.

It was an infringement of the one-child policy, but the rules weren't implemented so strictly in the city as in the countryside, where local officials often forced women to have abortions once they exceeded their birth quotas. Sam's parents moved to another district in Shenzhen, partly so that the neighbourhood party committee – the most local branch of government – wouldn't realise what had happened. Zhao's husband's colleagues knew, of course, but turned a blind eye. Less surveillance and intrusion from one's neighbours was one of the many privileges of becoming urban.

The autumn after her sister was born, Sam was due to start middle school. She had asked her parents to send her to board at a school on the other side of the city that had an impressive reputation for foreign languages.

Sam had scored a partial scholarship with her entrance exams, but even so, the fees were relatively high for the time, at Rmb10,000 a year. Still, her parents supported her. They thought that boarding school would be better for Sam's studies than sharing a small flat with a newborn. And Sam being away during the term times would mean that it would look to Zhao's neighbours as if she only had one daughter: the little one.

Sam's childhood passed quickly within the school grounds where she spent nearly all her time. During the holidays, when she came home, she'd watch football on TV with her parents. Like many families in Guangdong province, they had grown up watching the English Premier League because they could catch the television signal broadcast from across the water in Hong Kong. Sam's favourite team was Real Madrid, which she chose for its number of star players and success rate. She'd kick around a football sometimes with her primary-school friends back home, or on her middle-school pitch.

She got on well with her parents, especially her father, from whom she inherited a clownish sense of humour. She liked to make herself the brunt of the joke; in front of her friends, she was a bold, carefree tomboy. Her self-deprecation also served as a form of teenage subterfuge to hide the fact that she sometimes took things very seriously.

Sam felt most comfortable alone, reading books for hours on end. When she was home she studied furiously in her bedroom in their high-rise apartment. It overlooked a road that grew busier and busier over the course of her childhood. By the time she was preparing for her high-school entrance exams, a Nokia mobile phone stall had set up on the street below her window, and the rhyming couplets of the sales jingle it broadcast through its tinny speaker imprinted itself onto her brain as she filled in her practice papers.

———

It was probably the endless exam papers that had distracted Sam from noticing the rate at which her home town was changing. Her parents lived in the old urban district, in an apartment block filled with other government workers, whose daughters and sons also attended good city schools like hers. By the 2010s, her neighbourhood had gone from being the centre of the city to just one small part of Shenzhen's urban sprawl, connected by swooping highway overpasses and metro lines. It had also become a city of rich, middling and poor districts, all jammed next to one another.

That summer, when she was home from university, Sam walked them all in the stifling subtropical humidity in search of a representative cross section of subjects for the sociology department's survey. She was given a list of randomly selected addresses to visit.

In the first eighteen years of Sam's life, Shenzhen's population had multiplied almost eightfold to a staggering 10 million residents. In a city that large, a random selection of households was not easy to navigate. Up and down Shenzhen's hills, finding the right place to cross the triple carriageways, August air so thick with moisture that it resisted your body's movements, Sam arrived at each doorstop drenched in sweat and catching her breath. She sometimes travelled for an hour to find nobody at home or to be chased away. So whenever she finally managed to get inside a flat, Sam took a good look around.

She came across many households that were newly rich and had the furniture to show for it, as well as many apartments like her parents' that looked tidy and plain. But the first household to leave a strong impression was in one of the poorer areas of the city, in a neighbourhood she had never been to before. An old woman invited her in, sat her in a chair the likes of which her own parents would have thrown away long ago, and turned on the miraculous, creaking fan for her. She offered Sam a can of something cold from the fridge. She was the first person to be so hospitable.

In the same district, the next door she knocked on opened to a family of five adults squeezed into an apartment the size of her own living room, some ten square metres. The man of the house, who was not much older than her, stood holding his baby to his chest as she ran through her list of questions.

'On a scale of highly unsatisfied, unsatisfied, moderately satisfied, satisfied or highly satisfied, how would you rate your job at present?' she read aloud.

Without smiling, he scanned the teenager in front of him and replied: 'Did the Party send you to do this?'

Sam hesitated. She hadn't considered her relationship to the party much up to that point. Like all universities in China, Sam's was publicly funded and led by a party secretary. Good students were usually invited to join the Communist Youth League in high school, helping secure their future careers in the civil service, but Sam had gone to a liberal high school in a liberal era for Shenzhen, and hadn't considered a career inside the system.

'Not quite,' Sam replied awkwardly.

'I'm guessing they did send you, so let's just say we are completely, utterly satisfied with everything in our lives,' the man said. He answered 'highly satisfied' to all of her remaining questions.

———

When she was fifteen, Sam was admitted to one of the best high schools in Shenzhen, a three-hour bus ride away from her parents' home along the city's swerving hill roads. She boarded, as she had in middle school. The high-school campus was a universe in itself, filled with tennis courts, swimming pools, an endless library and, most importantly, an excellent canteen.

One of Sam's strongest subjects was English. Her high school used material directly from American elementary and middle schools. In English class, Sam watched documentaries from the Discovery Channel and TV shows like *Friends*. Her school recommended they improve their English by listening to the BBC and Voice of America. In the school holidays, she listened to whatever VOA recordings she could find on domestic platforms, since VOA itself was blocked by government censors. She also read the Chinese local newspapers and watched Central China Television, the state's mouthpiece. Its daily news broadcasts at 7 p.m. were compulsory viewing for her politics tests.

Sam liked the social sciences, but she found the school's compulsory politics classes boring and absurd. The only way to pass the multiple-choice exam was to learn answers by rote, because none of the answers made logical sense to her.

> Q: *The Chinese Communist Party believes in Marxism. What is this a demonstration of?*
> A: *That the Chinese people have freedom of belief.*

The explanation the textbook gave for this answer was: *Chinese people have the freedom of religion, Communist Party members have used their freedom to choose not to believe in any religion.* Sam had no idea how these words made sense together.

Shenzhen was the opposite of Communist nostalgia: it embodied the capitalist present. Its school curriculum was much lighter on Mao's revolution and much heavier on Deng's reforms than schools elsewhere.

One of Sam's favourite history teachers taught the dissolution of the Soviet Union, which happened just before Sam was born. He recounted to the class the speech in which President Mikhail Gorbachev proposed an end to one-party rule. 'Our ideal is a humane, democratic socialism,' Gorbachev told the Soviet Communist Party leadership in February 1990.

'What does this mean?' the history teacher asked. 'It means that pre-existing socialism was not humane or democratic.' It felt to Sam like he was making an important point, but she only came to understand it several years later, when she was at university.

Another of his lessons featured Nicolae Ceauşescu, the last Communist leader of Romania. A youth activist in the then outlawed Communist Party, he became totalitarian once in power. In December 1989, six months after Beijing's military opened fire on students and protesters in Tiananmen Square, Romanian secret police opened fire on students and protesters in the city of Timişoara. Within a week, Romanians revolted and Ceauşescu was convicted of genocide, then shot by firing squad.

Another of her history teachers was even more daring. He showed the class videos from New Tang Dynasty Television, a channel set up by practitioners of the persecuted Falun Gong religious sect who had fled to America. At that time, in the late 2000s, NTD broadcast political news that was banned from being played in China. But the discrepancy between the scandals that Sam's classmates saw on NTD and the bland optimism of the state media that they had been brought up on was too large to bridge. It was impossible to watch for too long without becoming overwhelmed. Students shared the videos among themselves, though they didn't overtly discuss what happened in them, and began searching for more videos online.

In the early 2000s, before the censors got their act together, it was much easier to jump the Great Firewall that blocks politically sensitive content. A school friend slipped Sam a USB disk with free software on it that allowed her to browse the uncensored foreign internet. It was called FreeGate, and had been launched in 2004, partly with funding from the US government. It was an early version of a VPN or virtual private network, which is nowadays an essential tool for bypassing the government censors.

For Sam, using FreeGate felt like entertainment more than education. It was a window into a bizarre alternate reality that Sam didn't delve into too deeply. The corners that she explored read to her like they were written by fanatics. There were websites made by exiled Falun Gong practitioners, which spoke of torture suffered by believers in China. To Sam, surfing with FreeGate felt like looking at pornography. Nobody had explained it to her, but she knew it was taboo.

———

'Do you want to see the definition of insane?' a school friend asked Sam one day.

He opened his laptop and showed her an online forum called Utopia. Its home page was cluttered with text and photo slideshows. A red banner at the top of the page carried the yellow hammer and sickle, the symbol of China's Communist Party, and the slogan 'Building a modern socialist strong nation, under the resolute leadership of the Communist Party'. These kinds of slogans weren't unusual, being on all the state media portals too.

But unlike the state media portals, a prominent photo of Mao adorned Utopia's home page. *How crazy that some people still hang Mao portraits in their homes*, Sam thought, looking at the impassive face stretched out on her screen. *How weird that some still refer to him as China's great liberator.*

Once Sam delved into the discussion threads it became very clear that, unlike the government websites, Utopia's Marxist slogans were not just for show. Founded in the early 2000s by bookseller Fan Jinggang and economics professor Han Deqiang as a 'patriotic website for the public interest', the forum had become a home for the Maoist old guard who had joined the Communist Party in the early days of the revolution. References made to the US were not to 'America' but to 'the American imperialists'. By the early 2010s it had become China's largest Maoist online forum, averaging half a million visitors per day.

Utopia had flourished in the late 2000s along with the growing popularity of Bo Xilai, the governor of the megacity of Chongqing in China's south-west, who had resurrected Mao's cult of personality. Bo was beloved by both social democrats and Maoists on China's wide 'New Left' spectrum for his 'Chongqing model', which centred on a call for 'common prosperity'. Bo's approach featured heavy investment in public infrastructure, a tax on private luxury homes amid an overall push for redistributive taxes, and the relaxation of *hukou* for rural workers moving into the city of Chongqing. He also organised public assemblies for singing Mao-era songs and conducted an anti-corruption purge of his political enemies.

The social democrats thought Bo would pave the way for European-left social policies, such as undoing the *hukou* system or providing subsidised housing for the poor. On Utopia, the Old Red Guard saw Bo's rise as a sign that China's Maoist faction was about to regain its voice after its long defeat during Deng Xiaoping's decades of market reforms. The optimism continued even after Bo's downfall in 2012, when Utopia was briefly shut down by web censors before springing back to life.

Utopia's founder Fan had been opposed to Deng's reforms, believing they soiled Mao's legacy. Fan criticised the wilfully forgotten negative impacts of the reforms, such as the mass lay-offs of state-owned enterprise workers in the 2000s, the commoditisation of health care and education, and vastly unequal access to housing. Fan's, and Utopia's, guiding principle was that, under Mao, 'people had more dignity, higher social status and better welfare'.

Sam didn't understand much of what was being discussed on the forum, but what she saw she found hilarious. Her home of Shenzhen had been ground zero for Deng's reforms, prided itself on its history, and celebrated the anniversary of his southern tour. She had seen the economic tide in Shenzhen rising throughout her childhood as the city transformed into a vast metropolis that housed the sprawling campuses of her private boarding schools. Why would anyone want to turn back the clock?

———

When Sam arrived at university to study sociology, she stumbled into a campus that was a hotbed of liberalism in the early 2010s, radical by Chinese standards. One humid June day, the professor drew the classroom curtains, and played a documentary about the massacre of students in Tiananmen Square. The students didn't have to be told why the curtains were drawn.

Sam's sociology and anthropology professors tried to bring the outside world into the classroom. One lecture course on civil society featured a different visiting speaker each week, mostly NGO workers and social workers, who would talk about their work on issues ranging from urban poverty to sexual violence. Although it was an optional course, the hall was always crammed to capacity with over three hundred students.

Listening to these speakers gave Sam the inkling that, no matter how small a part she played, she could improve society through her actions. In Sam's high school, the teachers had encouraged their students to amass academic credentials in order to be of use to society. But these speakers weren't academics; some of them hadn't even gone to university. They were practitioners and community organisers, and the pathways they described for making change felt more direct than the elite channels Sam had known before, such as donating money. The lectures made her want to learn more – and to do it outside the classroom.

Walking around Shenzhen for the sociology survey galvanised Sam further. The truth wasn't to be found in the survey results, she thought. The truth was on the streets.

7

Injecting kids with chicken blood
June

When June left her village in the mountains to attend university in a city half a day's travel away, for the first time in her life she could support herself financially without her sister's help. Knowing this gave her a new-found boldness.

In China's universities, students speak of 'small-town exam-prep kings' – the whizz-kids from poor places who face a sharp confidence knock when adjusting to the middle-class cultures of their universities. June knew she was the poorest girl in her dormitory. One of her dorm-mates came from a rich city family and had a small glass cabinet on her desk that she used to store her Dior and Chanel make-up. Yet June's confidence remained intact, because she was making money. She was proud to be the only girl in her eight-person dormitory who earned her own keep.

Every term, June gathered a crop of scholarships and prizes. Good grades came easily to her, even without putting in much work, and her teachers loved her. Being an undergraduate gave her the status to tutor schoolchildren in the city in her spare time. She had always been the one in high school that her classmates went to for help; she was patient and had an air of calm authority, seeming older than her years.

She signed up with a teaching agency that put her in touch with parents seeking private tutors. At the weekends, June went on home visits across the city. She set her hourly rate at Rmb100 – a lot for her, but not much for the parents, she thought. In one weekend she could easily make more than her sister made in a full week at the factory.

One of her maths students was in his final year of high school. Once, when she arrived at noon on a Sunday, she found the boy still asleep. She was shocked by his maths level: he didn't seem to have retained anything from his first two years of high school. When she asked him why, he replied that he'd been napping and daydreaming his way through his classes. June realised that rural kids simply ditched school and got jobs, but city kids knew how to scrape by while paying the minimum level of attention to remain in school.

The parents all felt extravagantly rich to June, and their kids seemed to fall into two extremes: very brilliant or very lazy. The children of businesspeople were likely to be left to their own devices, she thought, and given last-minute tuition just before their exams; their parents cared more about preserving their wealth and less about education.

A few weeks after June arrived at university, she came across an online post by a third-year student, asking for partners in a moneymaking project. The plan was to hold a kids' tuition camp over the winter holiday. About a dozen students turned up for the first meeting; June went along too, out of curiosity. That was where she met Gaolin.

Gaolin was three years older than June and went to a different university. He was studying to become a primary-school teacher. His patience with children extended to a straightforward generosity with all people. Gaolin had, in June's eyes, a 'cleanness of heart' that meant he put others first, much like her deceased mother. Very soon after they met, they started dating.

In contrast to Gaolin, June was someone who prided herself on not giving in to others' demands easily. After successfully co-running the winter camp, she started taking up leadership roles at several student societies. She focused less on her studies. Now that she had met the demands of nearly every exam life had thrown her way, she realised that textbook learning was not her ultimate passion. She wanted to make things happen.

Her boyfriend supported her in the most practical way. June's university made all students run about two miles every day as part of their physical education. To save June's time and energy, her boyfriend volunteered to run the two miles for her, keeping her phone in the pocket of his tracksuit bottoms so that the run would be tracked on the university's app.

At the end of his run, he'd go to June's canteen to get her a bowl of noodles, since he always worried about her working too late to eat properly. He'd deliver the noodles and her phone back to her dormitory.

Then he'd return to his own university campus, where he had to run his own two miles.

———

In June's first summer break, she took a job as a live-in tutor with a family on the suburbs of her university city. There was no university accommodation during the holidays, so the job meant she could stay in the city and continue taking other odd tutoring jobs.

The family lived in an enormous villa that glittered with chandeliers. It had the kind of surfaces that could shine, unlike the mud and cement of June's home in the village. There was a large garden – a rarity in Chinese cities, where nearly everyone lives in an apartment block. The cellar was filled with Maotai sorghum liquor, China's most famous brand that cost up to $200 a bottle. To June, having one bottle on display was a status symbol; having a cellar was faintly ridiculous. The boom had created a class of millionaires with bold taste in interiors. The Chinese term for the nouveau riche includes the word for 'earth', which also means 'unrefined': it brings to mind that, merely a generation ago, nearly everyone lived off the land.

The boy June tutored was a bright eleven-year-old preparing for an entrance exam to a highly selective middle school. His mother was a stay-at-home wife, an unusual role in a country where, until recently, women could not afford to not work. The father was a businessman who would yell at the live-in maid for not chopping his mushrooms finely enough. Though he never yelled at June, she understood that she and the maid belonged to the same class of people within the household.

The boy's classes went by quickly, so June had a lot of spare time on her hands. When she wasn't tutoring elsewhere, she would wander around the neighbourhood, which was pleasantly leafy, with paths shaded by trees from the summer sun. There was a riverside promenade and a golf course nearby. She wondered whether she would ever be able to afford a city garden with a swing.

————

In June's fourth and final year of university, she started asking friends who had already graduated for advice on job hunting. Being presentable at the interview was important, the older girls told her. You needed to look professional, like you had made an effort. June learned to apply make-up by watching video tutorials on Douyin, China's domestic version of TikTok, as well as Xiaohongshu, a platform popular with beauty influencers. To figure out which of the many promoted products to buy, she studied the items her rich dorm-mate was using.

June practised her make-up regimen: washing her face, dabbing moisturiser across it, and then smoothing out her foundation, which was ever so slightly lighter than her natural skin tone. When the foundation was dry, she applied powder to make the surface less greasy and remove the shine. Then, a highlighter pen to accentuate the nose bridge and cheekbones. Next came eyeshadow: a subtle nude pink dusted up to the brows, and a darker brown applied towards the outer corners of her eyes.

She dragged eyeliner in one unerring flick across her upper eyelids. She used another highlighter to accentuate her lower eyelids – which are known in Chinese as *wocan*, or 'sleeping silkworms', and signify the tenderness of youth. She used eyelash curlers and mascara, pouting with concentration. Finally, lipstick: reds and brownish-reds looked more mature; pinks were too girlish.

Armed with a full face of make-up and a stack of printed CVs, June went to her university's careers fairs. Her strategy was to apply for everything and see what happened.

———

Entering the job market in the middle of the Covid pandemic was unlucky. But June had given out hundreds of CVs, been to dozens of interviews, and ultimately received plenty of offers from both the private sector and state-owned enterprises. She decided to go with the former: she wanted a fast-paced role that could widen her horizons much more than she wanted a stable government job for life.

All of her offers were from her home province save one, from Beijing. It was from a rapidly growing education tech start-up that had been listed on the New York Stock Exchange, giving it an air of internationalism which made the company seem very cool to June.

In the early 2020s, the online education industry was booming. The conditions were ripe: Chinese universities were producing plenty of graduates who could become teachers, while families as remote as June's were receiving high-speed internet coverage. In 2020, the sector reached its peak of activity as school shutdowns across China led to unprecedented levels of demand for online teaching.

Parents were spending more and more of their wealth on their children's education. Nearly everyone wanted to get their children into academic higher education, but there were only places for around a quarter. In order to compete, parents 'injected kids with chicken blood', *jiwa*, the slang term for turbocharging children by piling on after-school classes. Education became increasingly *neijuan*, meaning 'involuted', an anthropological term that gained viral popularity in the late 2010s, meaning 'self-defeatingly competitive'.

At the same time, another form of *neijuan* was happening in the education technology sector. China's start-up world was experiencing a funding bubble, and, awash with cash, venture capitalists gave companies both the pressure and the marketing budgets to grow at breakneck speed. The investors, as always, wanted to make a profit from exiting the companies, which required them to publicly list on a stock exchange. The earlier you did it, the investors thought, the more likely you were to score a big initial public offering. The race was on to grow as big as possible, as quickly as possible.

To pull more parents in, China's top edutech start-ups converged on similar sales methods. Salespeople were the nice face of the company. The operating manual of one of the biggest start-ups recommended that sales staff, who were predominantly female, tried to befriend the mothers who would be making the purchase. Call them 'big sister'. Ask them how often their husbands come home, and commiserate if they're always away. If the buyer lives in a rural area, she's likely to be lonely. Call them three times a day to chat like a friend.

You might end up speaking to the rural grandfather of a left-behind child. Remind him that his grandson's life is precious; he only has one shot at the high-school entrance exam, and you wouldn't want him to waste it. (You might get him to reflect on how his own son wasted his chance at education, and how we are luckier now to have online resources for children.) If the grandfather needs a few days to borrow enough money from friends and family to afford the tuition fees, then give him the time, but be sure to call him regularly to check in.

Get as much information as possible about each household and their child so you know which market segment to categorise them in, and then follow more fine-tuned strategies. Ask the buyer what the child's biggest difficulty is at school. *Maths? Okay, no problem, big sister.* Be soothing – the buyer is likely to be anxious. (They had better be anxious.) *Don't worry at all, we'll find a way through this together. We'll speak to one of our dedicated educational experts, Teacher Li, who has a decade of experience in education, and we'll get back to you with a personalised plan.* Send them a headshot of Teacher Li and his CV. Teacher Li may or may not exist.

Call back after ten minutes. *Teacher Li recommends these summer courses to fix the surface-level issues you identified in our last call. However, he thinks your son is likely to have some fundamental issues with his mathematical abilities that will require longer-term correction, so we recommend you sign up for the autumn term as well.* At this point, the caller might ask: how much is it? *Great question! We have a special promotion right now, I can give you a 20 per cent discount if you sign up during this call.*

If they're not sold, the next morning, Teacher Li – or someone pretending to be him – will call. Teacher Li is the bad cop. Teacher Li will speak for ten minutes without interruption in a stern voice befitting someone with a decade of teaching experience. The mother will remember that all teachers are mean, that she was afraid of teachers when she was a girl, and that the correct attitude to have towards teachers is fear. Teacher Li will start off by asking: *How many more days of your son's life do you plan to waste while you're still making up your mind?*

While Teacher Li is berating the mother on the phone, the salesperson who called the day before will send her a sweet message, saying something like, *I hope you don't mind Teacher Li's style: he takes matters relating to education very seriously, given his years of experience. He was so concerned when I told him about your son yesterday, and he just wants to make sure you do the right thing for him. He's very invested in children, and he feels a responsibility to set them on a good path.*

If, at the end of all that, the mother still hasn't made the purchase, the salesperson will call again and say, in that same soothing voice, *Okay, well, let me know if you reconsider and I will try to see what I can do for you. After all, we will certainly fill the class.* The subtext: we will fill it with your child's competitors.

———

The edutech start-up's interview process was the most thorough of all the companies June had applied to. There were three rounds of interviews, as well as a week of online training where applicants were tested on everything from the history and values of the company to their operating procedures.

The process itself piqued June's interest: she liked the rigour of the hiring methods. It signalled a company that wanted to take a serious approach to management. When offered the job, June took it straight away.

When she told her sister over the phone, May immediately said it was a bad idea. She worried about something happening to June in a city where she had no friends or relatives, a day and night's train ride from home.

When June told Gaolin, she knew it would be tough news for him to swallow. By then, he had been working for two years in a secure civil service position, which carried the prestige that all government jobs do in small places. But he simply replied, 'Go for it, I support you. I just hope you'll have time to visit home often.'

June moved to Beijing in July 2020. Before she arrived, she had expected she would only be able to afford to live in a cramped underground dormitory squeezed in with other girls, like migrant workers do. She was ecstatic to find she could share a two-bedroom flat with a view of the glass-walled offices in Beijing's north-western tech hub. It was on the end of the subway line, a place that old-timers at the tech giants mocked for having no nightlife, but to June it was modern, and promised a new beginning.

There was only one moment of loneliness in June's first week. She had just finished work and was on her way to pick up the new household items she had bought from the parcel distribution station near her compound. Beijing's monsoon-like summer rain had arrived. Although the deluge happens every year, the city's drainage system is always caught off guard. The pavement outside Beijing's Software Park was streaked with water and filled with office commuters like herself: opening the Didi ride-hailing app, June saw over three hundred people in the queue ahead of her.

She had no choice but to cycle in the rain. She unlocked a shared bike with another phone app and cycled to the parcel station. Balancing her heavy boxes on top of the narrow basket with one hand and steering with the other, she cycled against the wind and rain back to her flat. At that point, she realised she had forgotten her keys.

Her flatmate eventually arrived home and let her in. The next morning, she woke up dry, warm and very happy with her decision to come to the big city.

———

June had almost no colleagues from her region, let alone a village like hers. But until she gave a presentation describing her early education, they couldn't guess her background. Now and again, someone would tease her about her inability to write characters with the correct order of strokes, or to remember the Pinyin romanisation of a word. Her colleagues saw these habits as funny quirks; nobody guessed that they were remnants of what June had missed in primary school.

June worked in the operations team of her edutech company, which was the real engine behind the whole process. The teachers who gave the online classes were the stars, but they were essentially actors, reading off the 'standard operating procedures' prepared by the backstage team.

But being part of the operations team in a consumer-facing tech company meant long and erratic hours: if anything was broken, if any customer was unhappy, you had to fix it immediately. One night, she was woken up at 3 a.m. by a phone call from her boss telling her, 'June, I'm just off the plane. Send me those documents now.' She left her phone on overnight in anticipation of moments like this.

June respected her boss and trusted him not to ring her for no reason. For her, having a good boss was of the utmost importance. She felt she had come to Beijing as a blank sheet of paper, waiting for someone to write onto her. Surely, in a city of such diverse talents, she would eventually come across another person like Teacher Song, an emissary from a world beyond her reach who could open a door to it.

The other graduates in June's team were at least five years older; she was the youngest and hungriest of the bunch, and her boss noticed her proactivity. He told her to attend other departments' meetings when they discussed staff promotions, so she would learn how the bigger operation worked. Then he started taking her to meetings with him.

Initially, she felt like an idiot, sitting there among the senior managers with nothing to add to the conversation. She felt like she ought to be doing something useful, like taking minutes, but her boss told her there was a secretary especially assigned to the task. He told her he simply wanted her to absorb the way they discussed things.

June was desperate to learn and grew anxious if she wasn't busy. The most difficult times for her were the lulls at the start and the middle of the school term, just after the busy period when the company went on a charm offensive to persuade parents to pay for the next set of classes. This busy period was the source of nearly all the company's revenue.

During the peak renewals season, the whole office would be working from 10 a.m. to midnight. But as soon as the rush was over, and June had a few weeks with little to do, she couldn't sleep.

'Just take it as a paid holiday. Have some rest!' her boyfriend Gaolin told her over the phone. But she couldn't rest. She worried that if she wasn't picking up new skills every week, then sooner or later she'd be replaced by a younger hire who was learning faster than she was. Beijing was competitive. Beijing was full of talent. June's colleagues, especially those who had grown up in Beijing and other big cities, radiated a relaxed confidence to a degree she had never seen before.

At the same time, Beijing was full of opportunities. There were many other companies that June could work for. That took away the sting of any setbacks: there was always another option. A friend back home once told her over the phone that she had been rejected after a job interview, and it had been a big blow. When June heard this, she thought how different she had become since she had started living in Beijing. At June's village primary school, if you lost your one best friend, you would feel totally alone. But in the big city, if you lost one friend, you had plenty of others. If someone didn't like her, it was their loss. She would have plenty more offers round the corner.

———

June's hours were perfectly mismatched with her boyfriend's. Gaolin worked from 7 a.m. to 4 p.m., while June was working on the edutech platform's after-school training programme: she started at 1 p.m. and often carried on until 11 p.m. For the first few months of their long-distance relationship, they barely spoke to each other.

An opportunity to meet up finally arose in October, when they were both on work trips in the same city.

'How do you think things are going with us?' she asked him.

'I don't think we can stay together if we're not in the same place,' Gaolin replied glumly. He knew that there had been other boys chasing June when they were at university, too. 'Beijing is full of so many impressive and outstanding people. You're bound to meet someone you like.'

'I'm sure Beijing is full of impressive people, like Xi Jinping, and it would be very cool if I bumped into a celebrity on the street, but it's not like they're going to start dating me,' June joked back.

Gaolin was hardly reassured. 'How will I find a job in Beijing when the competition is so intense, when all of these talented people already live there? What happens if I move there and I suck at my job, and then I find it difficult to get a job back home?'

June couldn't really empathise with these kinds of fears. Her own instinct – to reach past her own horizons to grab at something unseen – had only been reinforced by her life in Beijing. Big opportunities and pay cheques abounded, even for a fresh graduate in the middle of the pandemic-induced economic slump. The edutech industry was hiring tens of thousands of new employees every month.

'I'll help you find a job,' June promised Gaolin.

On the Sunday after they both returned to their respective homes, June rewrote Gaolin's CV and posted it on Boss Zhipin, one of Beijing's new job-listing platforms that connected the young professionals pouring into the cities with recruiters. The demand for these services meant that, within six years of its founding, Boss Zhipin's parent company was listed on the New York Stock Exchange at a valuation of over $10 billion. Every month, more than 8 million employers and would-be employees browsed its app.

By Tuesday morning, Gaolin had received several interview requests. As a young graduate with teaching experience from the kids' holiday camp he'd met June through, he was a hot prospect for the edutech industry. June wrote him a guide for responding to interview questions. By the end of the day, he had three job offers.

On Wednesday, Gaolin handed in his notice to the civil service. He wasn't very attached to the job itself, apart from it being a safe bet; he could see that he had little room for advancement, that promotion in the state system depended on seniority and being liked by his superiors, and that in those regards, his youth was a detriment. The next month, Gaolin moved in with June in Beijing, and started his new role as a private tutor on one of the city's big platforms. As an intern, he already earned twice what he had made back home.

8

The drop-out teacher
Siyue

Even after she had realised her private college on the outskirts of Beijing was a scam, Siyue wanted to make the most of it. Her parents had paid for the tuition out of the savings they had left after the stock-market implosion. Siyue was committed to mastering English – doubly so since she had gone against her father's wishes to study it. She knew she was good at teaching herself things but had started too late to score well on her university entrance exams. She wanted to find good teachers.

Siyue's college occasionally brought in guest lecturers from Beijing's many legitimate universities, and whenever that happened, Siyue would sit in the front row, looking for every chance to strike up a conversation with the teacher after class. Her boyfriend, Jiaolong, encouraged her to walk with them to the subway station, or ride the bus with them. She used such occasions to practise her spoken English.

But as the months passed, she felt these snatched opportunities were not enough for her to keep learning at the pace she wanted. Staying at the college, the best she could do was to *hun rizi*, to 'while away her time'.

At the end of her first year, she walked into the headmaster's office, told him she was leaving, and demanded her paltry deposit of a few hundred renminbi back.

'If you're going to kick up a fuss, I'll call the school guards on you,' he threatened her.

'You can try that,' Siyue bluffed, 'but all the boys in my class are waiting outside this office for me, and if you call the guards, I'll call them in to beat you up.'

Nobody was outside the door, but the headmaster fell silent. He thumbed through a few hundred renminbi notes – barely enough to buy food for a week in Beijing – and gave them to her.

———

Now Siyue needed to do two things: earn money and find a way to continue learning English. The first was more pressing. Jiaolong, who left the private college at the same time, convinced her to accompany him to his home town in Hangzhou, near Shanghai, where he wanted to hold a summer English camp for local primary- and middle-school students. Siyue took what was left of her savings to buy a ticket for the five-hour train ride to Hangzhou. She would help Jiaolong manage the camp and recruit English teachers.

It was the summer of her nineteenth birthday, and Siyue walked the streets of Hangzhou, pitching her 'Enjoy English' camp to parents and teenagers. She was back in the gently clouded south, away from the dust and solar glare of Beijing, walking the city that Marco Polo had once described as his favourite in the world. She wandered by Hangzhou's rivers and lakes, which reminded her of a more splendid version of her riverside village home.

In a few short weeks, she enrolled four hundred students. She left that summer with a feeling of satisfaction that she had learned to run a business, to speak better English, and had enough savings to propel her through another academic year in Beijing.

Except she had nowhere to study. The exams she had taken in the private college were useless: they weren't nationally recognised and so couldn't count towards a degree classification. If she wanted a qualification, she'd have to start again.

Siyue decided to enrol in the national programme of adult education degrees available to those who were too old for the standard university entrance exam. She went back to her old college and convinced her five former dorm-mates to join her. They dropped out together, and rented a flat near the campus of Beijing Foreign Languages University, the top English-teaching institution in the country, which administered the English adult education degrees. It was a cramped but cosy home: someone would always be making food, and they always shared it.

At the start of Siyue's second summer in Beijing, she prepared for another Enjoy English camp. This time she tried to recruit some foreign students at Beijing's universities to teach – it was the early 2000s, and these universities were opening up to foreign visitors. Foreign teachers commanded a premium in the eyes of Chinese parents, even if they didn't speak English natively or at all well. If they were white, that was close enough.

Siyue handed out flyers at the entrance of a university. Seeing one young white couple walking by, she crossed the road to catch up with them, and asked them to read her leaflet. The boy looked at her askance, but the girl took one. Seizing her chance, Siyue suggested they go to the nearby McDonald's for a coffee.

They agreed, and turned out to be exchange students from America. Siyue gave it to them straight. 'We don't have much money, so you'll have to buy your own train tickets to Hangzhou, but when you get there, we'll be able to give you this much in wages every week, and I'll take you out around Hangzhou and we'll have lots of fun. How about it?'

The couple accepted: they were in China to see more of the country, after all, not just Beijing, and they liked Siyue's honesty and directness. Siyue went back to Hangzhou to recruit students with fresh pride: she had scored two foreign teachers, and not just any foreigners, but native English speakers.

Siyue became very close to the American couple, and when the three of them returned to Beijing in the autumn, they kept meeting up on weekends. She'd pepper their conversations with questions about English, wanting to make sure she spoke as real people did, not in the imagined dialogues of the textbooks she had always distrusted. 'Siyue, your English is improving so much,' they'd praise her, and it was true: when they had first met outside of the gates of their university, Siyue had been much more hesitant in English.

Enjoy English's business boomed. It did so well that, the following year, the school they had rented space from got wind of how much they were making, banned their students from going, and put on their own rival summer camp instead. With nowhere else to host students, Siyue and Jiaolong had to give up on the camp.

Jiaolong pivoted to running a pearl business in Beijing, which Siyue helped with on the side. Jiaolong wanted her to go into business with him full-time, but Siyue's interests lay elsewhere. She was still young; she wanted to learn and have fun, not be a pearl-seller for the rest of her life. She felt Jiaolong was becoming increasingly controlling. Out of college, he seemed more focused on making money and more hard-edged.

Siyue remembers the exact moment she fell out of love with him. On a crowded bus, Siyue gave up her seat for an elderly lady, and then sauntered over to where Jiaolong was sitting. 'Now it's your turn to give me your seat,' she said, smiling at him cheekily. He looked back at her coldly. 'If you want to be a kind person, you stand,' he said.

At this point they had been a couple for four years and were living together. After another fight, Siyue went to stay with a friend for a week, and told Jiaolong to meet her after the week was up to discuss their relationship. He arrived wearing flip-flops, shifting his weight and gaze from side to side. A street guy, Siyue thought, someone who knows how to play the game. Perhaps he was in shock, or defensive, but he didn't show he was taking her concerns seriously. 'Let's just break up,' Siyue said. Jiaolong agreed offhandedly.

Only after Siyue moved out did Jiaolong realise that she had meant it. But by then she was gone.

––––

In 2007, Beijing was aflame with Olympics frenzy. The government began a massive drive to train half a million volunteers from across the country to speak English to the tourists that would descend the following summer. Since breaking up with Jiaolong, Siyue had placed all her focus on learning and teaching English, and had become a fairly confident English speaker with many of her own private students. She loved the idea of being part of the Olympics effort. She applied to Beijing's Olympics Organising Committee as a student volunteer, but her application was rejected because she didn't meet the minimum requirement of being a full-time undergraduate; since she had taken adult education courses, she wasn't part of the formal university system.

Other opportunities came round quickly enough. Siyue found a part-time gig teaching English at a tuition centre in a shopping-mall complex in the Central Business District, a few blocks away from the trouser-shaped Central China Television tower where she had once dreamed of working on the *Outlook* show.

Siyue's tuition centre was on the same floor as the offices of New Oriental, China's biggest private education company. Its young founders cracked jokes in public interviews and talked boldly about their dreams. Their idealism was all the more arresting in a country where private enterprises, and private ambitions, had only recently become legal.

When Siyue got out of the lift to her office, on her right was the pristine and well-lit reception of New Oriental, while on the left was her rather dilapidated tuition centre, seemingly always on the verge of going bankrupt. Every time she stepped out of the lift, she couldn't help but look across at the New Oriental offices and wish she worked there instead. One day, she went on over and asked if they had any vacancies for teachers, but the receptionist didn't show much interest. She made the mistake of sharing her ambition with her mother, who scoffed, 'You, a teacher? What would you teach at New Oriental, how to cook?'

Siyue heard one of the full-time teachers at the tuition centre was leaving for something better, but she felt she needed more experience before moving on. She started sitting in the back of his classroom, taking notes on his teaching methods, and they became friends. When he finally quit, they exchanged contact details. 'Please think of me if you ever have any jobs going,' Siyue said, 'I don't think this place is going to last much longer.'

Soon after, he messaged her: the Beijing Olympics Organising Committee was recruiting more English teachers for its university student volunteers. Did she want to audition?

Siyue had her hair done at a salon for the occasion but didn't have any class outline prepared. She turned up slightly late and improvised as she so often did in class. Looking at the rows of people in front of her, she pretended they were her Hangzhou students at summer camp. She tried her best to exude enthusiasm for her subject, and soon settled into a relaxed rhythm, asking her students to repeat after her.

Out of thirty teachers who applied, including much more experienced New Oriental teachers and TV anchors, Siyue was one of only two hires. She signed a contract on the spot for Rmb1,000 per day – an incredible amount of money to her.

Her first task was to teach a series of one-week intensive English camps for the Olympics volunteers. It took Siyue a long time to get rid of her feeling of inferiority to her students. They were from Beijing's universities, the best in the country, places she had never got close to entering. At twenty-one years old, she was younger than some of the students. But although their written English was much better than hers, the Olympics needed volunteers fluent in spoken English – Siyue's forte. She had honed it in conversations with people like the American friends she had met through Enjoy English.

One day, when she truly couldn't shake the feeling of being an impostor, she called the man who had hired her and told him that she felt she wasn't good enough for the job.

He listened calmly, and then said, 'Do you want to know why we hired you? It wasn't because your English was the best out of all the teachers who auditioned. It was because of our Olympics slogan: *Our volunteers' smiles are Beijing's best postcards*. We think you capture that spirit perfectly.' For the first time, Siyue was being told she could be a role model.

One of her last assignments for the Olympics took place on a sequestered military base far out on the outskirts of Beijing. The Olympics Organising Committee had assigned military drivers to chauffeur the international delegates arriving in Beijing, and they needed to welcome their passengers. The committee made a list of a hundred phrases – 'may I take your luggage?'; 'we are ten minutes away from the hotel' – that the drivers would be tested on after three months of her tuition.

Arriving at the base on her first day, Siyue walked into her classroom. One hundred men stood up in military synchronicity and started applauding her. She immediately turned round and left the room.

Outside in the corridor, she took a few deep breaths, then went back in.

As it turned out, her students were as intimidated as she was. Many of the men had left school at the age of fifteen or younger, and now they were tasked with learning enough English to speak to foreign leaders. Several of the soldiers approached her and confessed: 'There's no point bothering with us, we're not good at learning.' They didn't know the English alphabet, despite it being the basis for the Pinyin Chinese pronunciation system taught in the first year of primary school.

Siyue was years younger than these army veterans, but she understood how they felt: she, too, had been told by her schoolteachers that she was no good at learning, shamed in front of her class, dragged to the riverside by her mother and asked what she was doing with her life.

'We can learn one sentence per hour,' Siyue replied, projecting the confidence in them that she knew they needed to hear. 'That's thirty sentences each month. After three months, everyone will be able to pass the exam.'

At least once every class, she would walk through all the rows of the students holding a microphone for them to repeat an English phrase into. She knew there was a vast difference between being able to listen and being brave enough to speak. She tried to introduce some silliness to ease their nerves: when a soldier was too shy to say anything, she would ask for ten press-ups. After this made the soldiers laugh, they started to relax.

It was very different from the classrooms that the soldiers or Siyue had been in before, where a stern teacher would keep her distance from the silent students. Siyue persuaded her students to come to the front of the classroom, not to recite, but to put on little performances: a president getting into a car, a driver asking him for his luggage. She made up silly mnemonics for words like 'luggage', which could become *la ga'er*, the Beijing slang for the pull-out handle on a suitcase.

At the end of the three months, every one of Siyue's soldiers passed.

In Siyue's final assignment for the Olympics, she taught an intensive week-long summer camp for volunteers. She lived in the camp dormitories, where four teachers shared a room, and all the women shared a communal shower room, as was normal in schools and universities. She didn't like showering when there were lots of people around, so she chose the oddest times of day to do so.

One afternoon, as she went into the shower room, she was surprised to find there was someone else already there. She and the other woman had the same shampoo, so they made small talk for a while about that. As the other woman was leaving, she told Siyue that she worked for the New Oriental branch next to her old office and that they would soon be hiring again. The Olympics had ignited popular interest in learning English, and New Oriental was on the cusp of a huge expansion. Siyue washed her hair at rapid speed and immediately went to knock on the door of the woman's dormitory to get her mobile number.

After the camp was over, Siyue went back to that New Oriental branch for an interview, and this time she was accepted straight away.

9

The workers' centre
Leiya

Immediately after leaving the leatherwear factory, where she'd got sick of the creepy male boss, the rationed shower time and the daily rush from dormitory to warehouse, Leiya started the job she had lined up in another garment factory. Half of the girls from her dorm followed her; the other half went to a different factory.

Leiya's new factory was run by Hong Kongers. By then, in the mid-2000s, working hours had improved a little: in Leiya's new plant, overtime was capped at 9 p.m. each day, and they were guaranteed one day off every week.

For the first time in her working life, Leiya had free time. It was deeply uncomfortable. On her first day off, an unremarkable Sunday, she woke up not knowing what to do with herself. She didn't look for extra work to fill the time, which would've been her usual instinct. By then, she no longer had to send money to her parents. She had enough money for herself, but there wasn't anything she could think to spend it on.

Leiya, along with her dorm-mates, took to standing on the balcony that ran down the outside of all the dormitories on her floor, leaning on the railing and facing the world in a silent daze. She would stare blankly into space or watch the city below from her four-storey vantage. There wasn't much of a city view in the outskirts: she could see the roofs of the warehouses below, and, beyond, the factory gates, the mid-rise apartments where richer urban families lived, on streets dotted with people going to and fro. Going about their lives.

Leiya finally had time to think and ask herself what she really wanted from life. Whatever it was, she was sure it wasn't this: a life spent between the dormitory, canteen and factory floor. She and a friend toyed with the idea of saving up and opening a small shop. Becoming a business owner was the most obvious kind of freedom she thought might be open to her.

Her friends who had been at the factory longer were more advanced in their explorations of leisure. One had seen leaflets describing a venue where factory workers could go to socialise, play games and even sing karaoke – for free. She urged Leiya to go with her. After avoiding her friend's invitations for some time, she finally went with her to an event. A volunteer introduced the venue's work, the cultural events they held, the choir nights, the free library. Leiya thought it was surely a scam, and didn't go back.

A stretch of free time approached to taunt Leiya. For the week-long Chinese New Year holiday, Leiya stayed in the city, as she usually did. This was the time of year when workers went home to their villages and saw the families they had been sending money to all year. They would often quit their jobs to prolong the annual trip that made working far from home meaningful. But Leiya had no relatives to see back home – her parents and brother were in the city, and she didn't particularly want to see them either. She had spent very little of her childhood with her parents, who had left her to take care of herself and her brother after they went away to work in the city.

Leiya had nothing to do except take the odd overtime shift. The city was already emptying out from the steady exodus of workers in the month leading up to New Year's Eve. The soppy festival atmosphere and the thought of everyone returning to their family gatherings made Leiya's skin crawl.

On one of the first days of the New Year, Leiya got a call from an unknown number on her mobile phone and was so bored that she picked up.

'Hello,' a voice on the other side said, 'I'm calling from the City Workers' Community Centre. You came to one of our events last month . . .'

They remember me, Leiya thought with surprise. They noticed me!

'. . . so if you're still in the city, we thought you might like to come to some of the events we have planned over the holiday period . . .'

Leiya said yes, she wanted to go. She was meant to work overtime that evening, but she skipped it.

The community centre was the latest incarnation of China's long but troubled tradition of labour organising. The Mao-era workers' congresses lost their influence in the 1980s as the government sold off its state-owned enterprises. In the ten years after 1993, 50 million workers were laid off. Waves of unrest swept the country as the fired workers formed transient, informal organisations to demand owed wages and pensions.

By the time Leiya started working at factories in the early 2000s, the nature of labour organising had changed again. Protests were now moving to the private sector, where the majority of urban workers were employed.

These protests were particularly concentrated in the Pearl River Delta, home to the densest clusters of factories and migrant workers, including Leiya. In the mid-2000s, of over 200 million migrant workers nationwide, around 80 million were in the Pearl River Delta. Their most common problems were too much overtime, unpaid wages, workplace injuries and being without a labour contract.

When workers were unhappy, they quit, as Leiya had done in the leatherwear factory. Very few workers resolved their disputes through the formal trade union system. The Communist Party oversees all legally recognised unions in China. But these officially sanctioned trade unions are often controlled by the factory management. The party sees its goal of maintaining social stability as best achieved through suppressing workers' protests.

In the absence of effective unions in the workplace, labour activism pivoted to labour NGOs based in the community. By the late 2000s, there were over thirty labour NGOs in the Pearl River Delta, of which Leiya's community centre was one. They were founded by migrant workers and social workers, as well as academics from Hong Kong, just across the border.

Many of these NGOs gave legal assistance, helping workers claim workplace injury compensation and overdue wages. Community-based NGOs ran classes on labour laws, occupational health and safety, sexual harassment in the workplace, and other labour-related topics. The community centres often had libraries, a free-to-use computer, and social events. They were funded through a mix of donations, foreign foundations and charging fees for services. The concept of charitable organisations was new to modern China; it was easy for Leiya to assume getting something for nothing was a scam.

Soon Leiya became the one dragging her dorm-mates to socials at the City Workers' Community Centre, which was based in a rented apartment half an hour's walk from her factory. There was a karaoke system of sorts, fashioned out of a microphone and a CD player. People would stay late for their turn to let rip. Most of the events Leiya first attended were simply social encounters that provided her with a life and a sense of purpose outside the factory.

A year after Leiya spent her first Chinese New Year holiday at the centre, she applied to become a volunteer. In her first training session, the facilitator asked everyone to introduce themselves. When it was Leiya's turn to speak, she found she could barely open her mouth. Nobody had ever asked her to introduce herself in public before. She didn't know what she was meant to say. When she finally said her name, her voice shook.

Leiya felt both frozen and fascinated by the challenge of doing something so unfamiliar. As the weeks passed, she went from not being able to speak in public, to getting used to having an audience, to even organising and leading some events herself. She felt like she was stretching herself, and she liked that feeling.

A year after that first training session, Leiya decided that the centre might give her the life she wanted: a life where she could learn new things every week. She quit her factory job and started working at the centre as a full-time intern. When she told her factory managers, they were sure she had been scammed by the centre.

She moved out of the factory dorms and into a tiny flat in the dense migrants' settlement that had sprung up in the industrial outskirts of the city. These were called 'villages in the middle of the city' or 'urban villages', which referred both to their poverty and to their origins as agricultural villages that had been swallowed up by an expanding city. As the city grew, more and more migrants had arrived in these settlements and built tall, skinny apartment blocks, mostly without planning permission. The structures teetered a few storeys high, leaning in towards one another, leaving a thin sliver of sky over the narrow walkway below.

Although Leiya knew it was right for her to leave the factory, she often felt crippled by self-doubt. She knew she had come a long way, but she didn't think she had the skills to help those around her. The community centre opened at 1 p.m., so in the mornings Leiya enrolled on a computer skills course near the urban village. It was the late 2000s, and while few migrant workers had regular access to a computer, there was a wave of excitement for these new gadgets. Courses like the one she attended were popular with workers looking for a way up from the shop floor.

Her mother, who had finally found some financial security after seeking it for a lifetime, tried to talk her out of her decision to leave her well-paid factory job, but failed. Leiya went from making over Rmb1,000 a month in a job with guaranteed accommodation and a long-term contract, to making Rmb600 in an internship with shaky funding and an uncertain future. She had joined China's nascent world of labour NGOs.

———

At one of the social gatherings Leiya's centre organised, she met Chufeng, a technician at a local government office. Chufeng was one of the few regular attendees with job security and decent pay. He had started going to events at the City

Workers' Community Centre out of curiosity after seeing the crowds of people outside it on weekend nights.

Chufeng noticed Leiya in the centre's workshops because she asked so many questions. She was always learning something new, and Chufeng admired that. She was twenty when they met, and he was a few years older. He became her first boyfriend, and soon – but not soon enough – her husband.

Chufeng was different from the men Leiya remembered from her village, who were waited on by their women. Chufeng did lots of things on his own initiative – sweeping the floor of the community centre, washing dishes and cooking for large gatherings. In Leiya's village, households washed men's and women's clothes separately, because women were thought to be dirty. In the morning queue for the washbasin, the men washed their faces before the women. But Chufeng waited for Leiya.

After working at the community centre for two years, Leiya met the staff of a feminist NGO who had come to run a workshop at the centre. Although most of the migrant workers they served in the nearby electronics factories were women, Leiya was the only woman in the leadership of the community centre. Leiya hadn't talked about gender with her colleagues before. She knew that women's lives were unfair, but took for granted that that was their fate. After she attended the workshop, she felt as if she'd suddenly glimpsed a way forward: that the injustices of womanhood could be named and, what's more, be redressed.

Leiya left the workshop steaming with excitement, wanting to share everything she'd learned with her male colleagues, but they didn't seem so open. In fact, she suspected they felt threatened. When she raised the topic of gender, they started bemoaning their own problems in the social hierarchy as low-waged men from the countryside. 'Bride prices are so high nowadays, we need hundreds of thousands of renminbi to find a wife,' they said.

Leiya herself didn't believe in the traditional custom of the bride bringing her dowry to the marriage, or the groom bringing a bride price to the bride's parents. Nor did she let her parents get involved in her relationship with Chufeng, in case they demanded some form of bride price from him. After a few months of meeting Chufeng, Leiya became pregnant. At the end of their first year together, Leiya gave birth to a girl.

Leiya had not been that concerned about having her daughter, Xinling, outside of marriage. Under the one-child policy, a marriage certificate was required to apply for the birth permit from the local government that was then needed to get the child a *hukou*. Neither Leiya nor Chufeng had city *hukou* anyway, and took it for granted that their child would be in the same situation.

With her pregnant belly, Leiya was sometimes stopped on the street by neighbourhood officials looking out for infringements of the population controls. She held them off by promising she'd give birth back in her home town, ensuring they'd have one less case on their hands. In hindsight, she was lucky: she had a boldness borne of ignorance. A friend in the same situation later told her that she had been arrested and taken to an abortion clinic; her family had paid a bribe to get her out at the last moment.

Without a birth permit, Leiya couldn't give birth in a state hospital. Instead, some of Leiya's friends went to the local midwife, a barefoot doctor who worked without a medical permit from a rented apartment in the urban settlement with a few beds separated by curtains. For Rmb600, she would deliver your baby. For a hundred or so renminbi, she would do an illegal ultrasound in the fourth month of the pregnancy to tell you the sex of the foetus, and if it was a girl, you could pay extra for an abortion there and then.

But Leiya had always felt on the side of the girls, of the eldest daughters like herself who were given too much responsibility too early to take care of their younger siblings, and of the families back in her village who got bullied for not having male heirs. She wanted a daughter, and Chufeng was not the type to pressure her otherwise. After Xinling was born, Leiya's mother, who lived nearby, helped take care of her, and when she was old enough to go to nursery, Leiya would drop her off before going to the community centre.

——

Leiya wanted to do more work on gender issues, but her male colleagues at the community centre kept dismissing her plans. She contacted another NGO worker whom she had met at the feminist workshop and told her about her situation. 'Let's start something together,' Leiya said. 'We can't change the men, so let's go and work with women.'

Her friend agreed and, in the early 2010s, the two of them rented a space in a nearby industrial zone called the Garland District, where 100,000 women workers lived together in densely packed apartments. At lunchtime, in the long corridors of the apartment blocks, women would squat on the floor with their backs against the walls to eat from their lunch boxes, leaving barely enough room for someone to walk down the middle of the hall. The cement floors were coated with cooking oil from the hundreds of lunches eaten there. At the weekends, when workers had time off, the streets were packed with people having fun.

Leiya registered her new centre as a company: the Garland District Women's Centre. Many labour organisers would do this to avoid the process of registering an NGO, which perversely requires the backing of a government agency. Leiya started organising social activities like the ones she had first encountered at the community centre in the early 2000s: karaoke parties and film nights. But although the youngest women in the factories were only eight years younger than her – she was twenty-four by now – she felt like they came from a different generation entirely.

Most of the younger workers had smartphones and mobile internet subscriptions, and chatted to their friends through the QQ messenger app, a precursor to the WeChat app that dominates Chinese life today. They got their news and entertainment online. In Leiya's pre-mobile internet existence, all she saw every day was the factory interior, and going to fun events at the local workers' centre had given her a rare injection of outside joy. But the young women she met in the Garland District had different needs. Karaoke nights on a portable CD player didn't impress them as much.

On the other hand, they were much more aware of the raw deals they were getting at work. In 2008, China's Labour Contract Law came into effect. The government wanted to bolster the protections that had been outlined in the 1994 Labour Law, but poorly implemented. The country's reliance on cheap labour was becoming unsustainable. The number of young rural migrants pouring into cities was starting to drop. China's leaders wanted to shift the economy towards a higher-tech, higher-productivity model that didn't rely on a reserve army of cheap rural workers. At the same time, after two decades of breakneck change, the government started to worry about social harmony, and increased worker protections to quieten discontent.

The drafting of the Labour Contract Law was much discussed across China, both in the boardrooms of the foreign businesses who opposed it and on the factory floors. After the law was enacted, the government launched a massive publicity campaign that brought about a new awareness of labour protections. More workers started bringing forward claims against their employers. In the first quarter of 2008, the number of cases accepted by labour courts in the Pearl River Delta doubled from the same period the previous year. Now women came to Leiya's centre armed with questions:

My boss won't let me resign – he says he won't give me my month's wages if I do.
I got fired because my boss found out I'm pregnant.
I'm seven months pregnant and my boss keeps making me do night shifts.
My factory won't pay our social insurance contributions, is that illegal?

Rather than focusing on social activities, Leiya started to organise workshops on the topics most in demand: reproductive health, how to negotiate with managers, how to get maternity leave, and the importance of social insurance contributions. She also started to pivot towards providing legal support, giving talks on the Labour Contract Law based on what she had gleaned from it online. When she had been a factory worker, she had had no idea what her legal rights were, or where she might read about them. The mobile internet had changed all of that.

Although the women who came to Leiya's centre had a general awareness that they had legal rights, they still spoke in the language of fear and obedience. When they began their stories with 'The boss says . . .' Leiya would fire back, 'But what do *you* say? We've all been trained to be good, obedient children. But what do *you* want, what do *you* think?'

She coached them to negotiate with their managers. The Labour Contract Law was still very fresh, and labour organisers in the Pearl River Delta had great hopes for it. They believed that if the budding workers' movement had the law on its side, they couldn't go wrong.

10

The limits of the system
Sam

A screw fell to the ground
in this dark night of overtime
vertically plunging, lightly sounding
not attracting anyone's attention
just like last time
on a night like this
when someone fell to the ground
　　　　　— Xu Lizhi, poet and Foxconn worker

In 2012, in Sam's second summer break at university, she saw an advert for a summer school on labour studies circulating on social media:

The Labour Research and Practice Workshop

The dust has yet to settle on thirty years of reforms. China has already become the 'world's factory' as well as the 'world's construction site'. Migrant rural workers are the new subjects of this period of history, bearing the weight of the contradictions and difficulties that accompany China's path towards globalised capitalism. They have also

undertaken the great mission of writing the history of
China's social transformation. China's future is intimately
interwoven with this working class of over 200 million . . .

Headlining at the week-long workshop were famous professors
from Peking University, Tsinghua University, Renmin
University and Sun Yat-sen University, as well as universities
in Hong Kong and Taiwan.

The workshop was divided into two parts: theoretical study
and social practice. The initial study period included class
formation theory, as well as a survey of China's twentieth-
century workers' history from pre-revolution to Reform and
Opening Up. After the study period came a month's 'social
practice'. The application process was rigorous: after being
sent a reading list, students had to submit a 3,000-word essay
to qualify.

Sam applied, thinking the course would further her interest
in social inequality sparked by the previous summer's survey
work. Plus, it had big-name academics on board. Her parents
approved: it was free, and was held on the campus of Peking
University, which made it all the more prestigious.

Sam was accepted, and she bought the cheapest train ticket
she could find up to Beijing. She'd missed out on the sleeper
booths, so instead she sat on a hard seat for the 22-hour
journey from Shenzhen. It was by far the furthest she had
ever travelled on her own.

At the summer camp, she and a group of fifty other students
were introduced not only to labour scholars but also to NGO
leaders and activists. At the end of the week, they were given
options for continuing their research through practical
work: doing a social investigation, interning at an NGO, or
embedding themselves in a factory.

Having lost faith in the possibility of getting to know society through survey data, Sam wanted to see factory working conditions up close. She wanted to understand the assembly line from an anthropological perspective. Back home in Shenzhen, she applied for a job at Foxconn.

Foxconn, China's largest employer, is most famous for being Apple's main assembler of iPhones. Two years before Sam attended the labour studies workshop, in 2010, a series of young workers tried to kill themselves by jumping off the buildings in its flagship Shenzhen factory campus. A total of eighteen people in their late teens and early twenties jumped. Fourteen died.

The spate of suicides sparked an urgent coalition of students, academics and activists mobilising around labour issues. A group of Chinese sociologists wrote that the suicides should be seen as 'loud cries for help from the new generation of migrant workers'.

The scholars and activists were spread across mainland China, Hong Kong and Taiwan. The three regions were tied together by a globalised supply chain, where Taiwanese bosses with foreign investors in Hong Kong ruled Chinese workers.

Many of these student-scholar-activist groupings had worked together before on undercover investigations into multinationals in China such as Coca-Cola and Disneyland Shanghai. Now the summer's horrific, gradual unfolding of suicides brought them closer together and gave them a single target to organise around – Foxconn.

———

The Foxconn recruiter took a hard look at Sam, then read her ID card, which displayed her home address in Shenzhen's richest district. He waved her away. Following the string of Foxconn suicides, a group called Students and Scholars

Against Corporate Misbehaviour (SACOM) had been sending students onto the assembly lines as undercover investigators. Maybe she reminded the recruiter of one of them. Everyone knew that city locals didn't work on the assembly lines, and he could tell that this one wasn't used to intense labour: with her round face and bookish aura, Sam often looked even younger than she was.

Instead, Sam settled for volunteering at a labour NGO that she had been introduced to at the summer camp. It was a legal advocacy group that helped individual workers understand their legal rights and apply for compensation.

Every weekend when Sam went to volunteer at the NGO, she followed a gutsy teaching assistant from the summer camp whom everyone respectfully referred to as the 'Big Sister of the School' (*xuejie*) – the term of address for older female students. Big Sister dragged Sam and the other interns around hospitals in Shenzhen, carrying a bag of leaflets that outlined workers' rights to workplace injury compensation.

In Chinese hospitals, it's fairly easy to walk straight into a hospital ward, which hold four or more beds to a room, and have various family members traipsing in and out of them. Because of the under-resourcing of the public hospital system, family members tend to take on the bulk of inpatient care themselves, camping in the wards overnight on makeshift beds. Amid the constant commotion, nobody seemed to be bothered by a pack of university students wandering around. Big Sister and her interns went into the surgery wards in the hospitals around the Longhua district, where Foxconn's flagship campus lies, looking for patients with work-related injuries. For several weekends, Sam spoke to plenty of workers, but saw nothing more gory than amputated fingers.

One day, Big Sister decided they needed to try a bigger hospital. Striding into one of the open wards at Shenzhen Number 2 People's Hospital, Big Sister asked the whole room: 'Any injured Foxconn workers?'

The patients in the ward answered eagerly: 'Yes, there's one next door. Are you journalists? Go quickly!'

In the ward next door, Sam came upon a very tall man in his twenties, who was looking vacantly into the air. When he saw Sam, a crooked grin came over his face, the left side of his mouth frozen in an upward twist. Sam took out her student ID to introduce herself, and he started trying to grab at it with his left hand, his right arm limp by his side. In the corner of the room, someone who introduced himself as the man's father enthusiastically waved Sam over to sit down.

The tall man's name was Zhang Tingzhen. His father told Sam that Zhang had been injured the previous October while working for Foxconn. He'd been there for a month or so, and hadn't yet finished the trial period of his contract. He was an electrician, a skilled position earning Rmb4,000 a month – much more than entry-level assembly-line workers. Although he was working in the Longhua headquarters in Shenzhen, Foxconn had routed his labour contract to a subsidiary in the small nearby town of Huizhou, possibly to avoid paying higher social security in Shenzhen.

One day Zhang had been standing on a tall ladder and fixing an electric light on an external wall of the factory. While he was in the middle of his repairs, someone inside the factory mistakenly switched the electricity on. Zhang instantly received an electric shock and fell four metres, hitting the ground head-first.

It took an hour and a half after his fall to get him to hospital. By then so much blood had pooled inside his head that the doctor who saw him decided the only course of action was a partial lobotomy. By the time his parents and sister arrived from their Guangdong village, the operation was already over.

Zhang was moved to a bigger hospital for his recovery. In the X-ray scans of his head, his brain was the shape of the white yang half of the Taoist symbol, the black yin side cut out. Dark dots in the centre of his brain marked the dead cells.

Zhang was partially paralysed. The doctor warned his family the outcome of his brain damage would be terrible: he would be left with the IQ of a toddler. Zhang's father went to Foxconn to plead for compensation. But because his contract wasn't with Foxconn's Shenzhen plant, the factory initially avoided giving him any compensation at all. In order to fight for Zhang's rights, his father, Zhang Guangde, spent enormous amounts of time and effort visiting various courts and government departments, each of which would kick the ball to another.

'My whole family has been ruined by Foxconn,' Zhang's father told journalists. 'They don't answer my calls. They don't respond to my questions. They don't pay the medical bills. All they do is refuse to take responsibility.'

Eventually Foxconn started paying Zhang's parents a monthly allowance of Rmb11,000 plus treatment costs. But by the summer of 2012, some nine months after Zhang's injury, Foxconn was sending his father text messages demanding he remove his son from the hospital.

Foxconn told the media that it was justified in sending the messages, and claimed that under Chinese law Zhang had to undergo a disability assessment before getting medical compensation. In fact, this was not true – seriously injured workers can be in treatment for up to two years before receiving such an assessment. And because of the way Foxconn had structured his contract with its subsidiary, Zhang would have had to travel for two hours to Huizhou for his assessment, which was near-impossible in his state.

Foxconn lowered the price of its medical settlement by a third by claiming Zhang worked for the Huizhou subsidiary where his contract was based, although Zhang had never set foot there, and it was almost a couple of hundred miles away from the site of the accident. Eleven months after his injury, Zhang's family had accumulated Rmb200,000 in debt to pay for medical and other expenses. According to his father, that debt was much less than the amount Foxconn saved by claiming Zhang was employed in Huizhou rather than Shenzhen – Rmb300,000.

Meeting Zhang and his father sparked deep doubts in Sam's mind. In her textbooks, she had learned that Chinese citizens were equal before the law. At that point, despite years of Marxist slogan-reciting in her compulsory politics classes, she had never thought in terms of the power of 'capital' versus 'labour', but Zhang's case against Foxconn startled her with the size of the gap between the vast multinational and the injured man.

Sam had read the stories from the past few years about the Foxconn suicides and the suicide nets going up. But what struck her about Zhang was that he wasn't a minimum-wage assembly-line worker with no hope in his future. He was a skilled technician with a loving family from the countryside and hopes of marriage. He was the kind of person Sam's father could've been.

One year after his injury, Zhang's parents and Foxconn's representatives met in a labour arbitration in Shenzhen. His parents, fearing Shenzhen's lawyers would be in the pay of the city's largest taxpaying company, brought a lawyer from their home province of Henan. When the Foxconn lawyer arrived, the parents pelted him with eggs. Finally, Foxconn's Huizhou subsidiary agreed to pay the difference between the work compensation rates of Huizhou and Shenzhen.

At least Zhang had some kind of contract, and received compensation in the end. Labour NGOs estimated that in the early 2010s, four out of ten workers in China had no medical insurance at all.

After meeting Zhang, Sam felt it was not enough to go around hospitals giving pamphlets to injured workers. She started to think that there were things that couldn't be resolved through the system.

———

During Sam's fourth and final year at university, she attended a lecture by a visiting sociology professor from Hong Kong named Pun Ngai. Pun spoke about her research on the working conditions of women migrants in Apple's supply chain.

In one presentation, she showed a series of adverts from private clinics targeting female factory workers with promises of 'safe' and 'pain-free' abortions. Together with a lack of access to information about contraception and reproductive health, migrant women were prone to health complications from having several abortions in quick succession. Private clinics underplayed the risks of the procedure and preyed on migrant women's unfamiliarity with the city's inaccessible public hospital system.

'These adverts are a result of the commoditisation of female bodies,' Pun argued, referring to women migrants' experiences both on the assembly line and on the operating table. 'In this regard, the socialist *danweis* or work units of the past were a good solution: they included health care for all workers.'

From the history books that Sam had read in her Shenzhen schools, she remembered only the mistakes of socialism. But Pun, a famous professor whom she admired, was praising socialism's achievements. The contrast made Sam wonder what else she had missed in her education so far. She'd had the best schooling China had to offer, but she suddenly felt there was a lot more beyond the walls of her campuses.

By the time Sam finished university, the labour studies summer school she had attended in Beijing had closed down, as it had become too politically sensitive to advertise. But many of the students who had passed through that summer camp became organisers of workers' advocacy groups on their own campuses. In the top two universities in the country, Peking and Tsinghua, students had been running Marxist student societies registered as official university societies for decades. In the mid-2010s, the groups reoriented themselves towards activism.

This generation of students was born in the nineties and had come of age during the economic boom. Now, in their twenties, they were seeing widening inequality and the accumulation of social problems inherent to an economy that relied on disenfranchised migrant labour. Some of them were of the first generation in China to be born into well-off urban households and harboured their own class guilt. During a lecture on migrant workers, one student, Shen Mengyu, asked Peking University professor Lu Huilin: 'Professor Lu, are university students like us beneficiaries of the system?'

The Peking University Marxist Society ran a mixture of reading groups of texts by Marx and Lenin, and became acquainted with workers on campus by hosting social events for them such as film nights. During the university holidays, the society organised fieldwork trips for undercover work, where students would go to factories to work alongside migrant workers. They paired the students up and gave them backstories: so-and-so was a younger cousin who had flunked university and now needed to earn money. Afterwards, students would write about their experiences for the group to discuss. In a way, it was the most immersive sociology course one could have designed.

But treating such trips as academic research was frowned upon by the Peking University Marxist Society leaders; the goal was to truly transform oneself, to 'melt into the masses'. That promise of transformative group liberation was extremely appealing to some students. It promised them that, regardless of their background, they could become anyone.

———

Sam went on to graduate school to pursue a master's degree in sociology. Not long after she arrived, one of her lecturers invited her to join a departmental reading group on Marx's *Capital*.

Before that year of wading through the dense text, Sam had held broadly left-liberal concerns, but had yet to develop an overarching belief system. Reading *Capital* gave Sam her first complete theoretical framework. After a year of the reading group, Sam started calling herself a Marxist.

Another transformation was also taking place for Sam. Among her new reading-group classmates and professors, she shed some of the light-hearted humour that she had carried throughout her school years, when she had liked to joke and laugh during heavy discussions. She suddenly felt frivolous and superficial, like she had previously been a drop of oil on water, floating above the depths. These were serious people doing the serious work of researching a revolution, and Sam felt that she should adopt a more serious disposition in their presence also.

What her new-found Marxism entailed was less clear, because there was no recipe for revolution in Marx's writings that suited China's modern stage of development. *Capital* was a book that seemed to Sam to be simultaneously from the past and from the future. It had inspired China's revolution of 1949, but the legacy of that revolution was at once ubiquitous and indiscernible. China had never officially renounced its Marxism, of course, but was now governed by authoritarian capitalists. If the new generation of Marxists wanted a new Communist revolution, they needed to wrestle with the question of how China could avoid repeating its own history.

The answer, Sam came to believe, could be found through gathering the stories of the workers who had lived through the revolution of 1949. This generation, a little older than Sam's grandparents, was a precious resource for those studying Communist regimes. Unlike the young Marxists in most other countries today, young Marxists in China grew up alongside elders who have lived through revolution.

As part of her master's studies, Sam had read the American sociologist Joel Andreas's research on the governance of Communist-era state-owned enterprises, based on interviews with this generation of workers. He found that the Communist Party had initially experimented with democracy in the workplace, until its appetite for top-down control eventually eroded workers' power. Sam decided to pursue a similar approach for her master's thesis.

The window of opportunity to speak to those who had been adults in 1949 was shrinking: by the time Sam was doing her research, such workers were already in their eighties. For her fieldwork site, she chose a residential compound in Shanghai that was home to the retirees of a major shipyard that was nationalised during the Communist Revolution.

Conducting interviews did not come naturally to Sam. She took time to warm up to new people. Apart from her survey of Shenzhen in her first summer home from university, she had never had much need to speak to strangers; her parents had only moved house once during her childhood within the same city, and her school life, from primary school to her master's degree, had been wrapped in stable configurations of classmates and local friendships.

In Sam's first fieldwork assignment as an undergraduate, she spent several days at the same site without working up the confidence to speak to anyone. After that, she called an older classmate for help.

'Every morning, go to the same congee shop and order the same thing. By the third or fourth morning, the owner will remember you and he'll be curious enough to strike up a conversation himself,' her classmate told her. It worked.

Sam knew that her chosen academic career, in anthropology and sociology, meant overcoming her fear of fieldwork. It was not all terrifying: she took joy in exercising her curiosity and in being surprised by her interviewees. She and her classmates also supported one another by debriefing their fieldwork experiences together.

By the time Sam came to write her master's thesis, she was more experienced in the art of approaching strangers. On the whole, the retired Shanghai shipbuilders were a very easy crowd. They saw Sam as a baby-faced student, younger than their own grandchildren, who had endless time to listen to their stories. In the warm days of early autumn, Sam could walk straight into the unguarded compound and speak to the retirees as they sat in the pavilion, fanning themselves and shooting the breeze as they had every summer and autumn for as long as any of them could remember.

The workers Sam spoke to had migrated to the city from the countryside at a young age with their parents. Their childhoods and early adulthoods had been marked by various hardships: the humiliation of the Japanese occupation of the 1940s, the desperate search for work, the bullying by local gangs and mafia, and the corruption of the Kuomintang government that had formed China's first post-imperial Republic, and was then locked in a civil war with the Communist Party.

Some of the shipyard workers had been unemployed when the Communists took power in 1949. They had applied for jobs to the Communist Party's newly established Shanghai Unemployment Aid Committee, and been assigned to the shipyard.

These workers told Sam of the intense hope they had felt for a better life. After the revolution, their lives were 'turned around' by the state. The factory trained the new recruits for six months in technical skills such as making blueprints and welding. All the workers became permanent employees of the state-owned enterprise, which gave them dormitories, canteens, nurseries and schools for their children, and a health clinic. Moreover, they held the social respect of being skilled urban workers. As one told Sam, 'We really cherished our work then, and we loved our factory as if it was our home.'

Decisions on the workshop floor were made by the workers themselves in accordance with their experience and skill levels. Sam pored over the annals of the factory, which recorded the debates on how to create a 'million-ton' hydraulic press, a vast and complicated piece of equipment.

For Sam, the discussions recorded showed how ordinary technicians were listened to by the party cadres and factory directors, among whom they enjoyed a relatively equal status. Speaking to these workers brought to life the theories Sam was learning about in her *Capital* reading group. She reflected that the shipyard was the opposite of the Foxconn assembly line: in the shipyard, the workers held the skills and thus were masters of the production process, whereas on the assembly line, the machines held the technology and the workers were merely cogs.

But despite the high social status of the workers, they lacked formal power. The shipyard's director was appointed by higher-level party authorities, and so on up the chain. As a result, Sam concluded, workers' democratic participation in enterprises easily disintegrated during Deng Xiaoping's market reform era of the 1980s. By that time, the shipyard was hardly a worker-directed socialist enterprise any more; it was being governed by the party in a top-down fashion.

The shipyard went through 'shareholding reform', where the management became its sole owners, after buying out the workers' stakes at low prices. The workers had no say in the process, and many were laid off.

For some it felt like a betrayal of the revolution they had lived through. One afternoon during Sam's fieldwork, one of the shipbuilders told Sam his experience of the 1949 revolution, when he was unemployed and desperate for work. He recalled a crowd of young jobseekers listening to a local Communist Party activist giving a speech.

'Why are your lives full of bitter labour?' the activist asked.

'Because our destinies are bitter,' the crowd replied.

'It's not that your destinies are bitter,' said the activist, 'it's because you're being oppressed by the "three great mountains": imperialism, feudalism and capitalism.'

The shipbuilder said to Sam: 'Isn't that still the case for many workers today?'

———

The shipyard workers spoke in turns of phrase that reminded Sam of the Maoists of the Utopia forum that she had mocked in high school. Though she had thought those online Maoists ridiculous, she was moved by the accounts of the shipyard Maoists. The former shipyard union leaders spoke of the early years of the Communist Revolution with a clarity that made Sam feel the eighty-year-old workers possessed a stronger sense of conviction than she had ever felt in school.

Sam's fieldwork renewed her desire for social change, as did conversations with her classmates in the Marx reading group. One winter, they discussed the beating to death of Zhou Xiuyun, a migrant worker and mother who had been trying to get her unpaid wages, by the police in northern China. One officer had stood on Zhou's hair for an hour as she lay unconscious on the frozen ground. Sam and her classmates railed against the injustice of a system where migrant labourers were routinely abused by their employers and treated as second-class citizens by the government. China's workers were wealthier than they had been under communism, but they were now being exploited under an authoritarian capitalism.

In the conclusion to her master's thesis, Sam wrote that the Communist Party of China had 'already deteriorated into an exploitative elite alliance that commits massive expropriation of ordinary workers and peasants'. She argued that society needed to move 'beyond the inhumanity, inequality and indignity of capitalism in all its myriad forms'. By now, Sam was not only a Marxist but had reached her starting point as a Maoist: the need for revolution.

Part Three

II

How to build a school
Siyue

The year after the Beiijng Olympics, after Siyue joined New Oriental as a part-time teacher, the state broadcaster CCTV began talking to her firm about buying a package of English classes. CCTV had started broadcasting an English channel in 2000, called CCTV-9; the channel had even ventured into the US cable market. After CCTV-9 pulled off its coverage of the Beijing Olympics in 2008, the station prepared to relaunch the channel as a bigger news service that would tell the 'China story' to the rest of the world. The network is now known as CGTN, China Global Television Network.

Siyue was dispatched to give the CCTV anchors a trial English class. In the end, the network didn't approve the budget for the New Oriental package, but they offered Siyue a full-time job.

As a teenager, Siyue had watched CCTV's English programmes and dreamed of being on air with the worldly and confident young women who hosted them. Her mother had mocked her aspirations. But then again, her mother had also laughed at her ambition of becoming an English teacher after dropping out of college. She accepted the job and became an interpreter, sometimes even appearing on-screen.

CCTV is not only the country's main television channel, but also a state enterprise under the direct supervision of the central government, making it a prestigious work unit. For the first time in her life, Siyue had a complete employee package of social and medical insurance, and a dependable full-time salary.

When her mother used Siyue's company-issued social-insurance card to withdraw money in her home town, far from Beijing, she'd enjoy a rush of pride when the bank teller would look at Siyue's account details and say, 'Ah, your daughter is at a central state enterprise?'

Word got around their village, and suddenly, Siyue's family found that old feuds fell away and the neighbourhood bullies stopped bothering them. Even the shadow of her father's old lawsuit against the government felt lighter.

Working at the state broadcaster created an aura of privilege that Siyue could use to get things just by mentioning her employer. One year, her mother had wanted to build an additional house on their plot of land, but the local government had refused to grant her a building permit. When the village party secretary visited Beijing for the annual 'Two Sessions' political convention, Siyue gave him a call. She addressed him affectionately as 'uncle', the catch-all term for male family friends. She asked him how his journey had gone, asked after his family, and casually mentioned that she was in Beijing too, yes, working for CCTV. She didn't mention her mother's request for a building permit, but by the time the party secretary returned to her home town, the permit was ready. All he needed to know was that she was someone.

But merely being someone was not enough for Siyue; she wanted to do something. She couldn't bear the idea that she might ever interpret something less than perfectly, so she did a lot of preparation for each session, staying late at night and coming in on weekends. In her first two years, with the daily demands of having many colleagues to serve, her interpretation skills improved immensely.

Siyue's devotion to work didn't leave her much time for anything else. But one afternoon in the office, when she was feeling particularly in need of company, she went through her phone contacts list and wondered who she could ask to dinner.

Almost at the end of the list was Xav, a guy she'd met a year ago at a party she hadn't wanted to attend. That night, coming home exhausted from work, all Siyue had wanted to do was to curl up and sleep, but her then boyfriend had dragged her along to the party anyway. She had opened a can of Coke and placed it on the backrest of the sofa she was sulking on.

'That's not a great place to put a can of Coke, mate,' said the man sitting at the other end of the sofa. His northern English accent and dry tone made Siyue laugh. They started talking, and immediately clicked. They swapped phone numbers, and then Siyue got up to dance.

Later, after they had started dating, Xav told Siyue he'd lost that phone, and the only thing he had missed about it was her number. Thankfully, she had been the one to call.

——

Siyue came to feel that she and Xav were two people sharing the same soul. Conversations were so fluid, and they always had so much to talk about. Both Xav and Siyue were phenomenal linguists, and fascinated by the other's language: in the evenings, Siyue would often be reading an English novel on the couch while Xav sat next to her with a Chinese one.

Xav was a natural explorer, and although he hadn't lived in Beijing for as long as Siyue, he knew its nooks much better than she did. In their first few months of dating, Xav organised every date as a surprise, taking her to a restaurant in a *hutong* alleyway she'd never walked through before, or bringing her to the highest hill in Ritan Park at sunset, where they were alone, looking out at the skyline of the Central Business District. Xav liked to travel, backpacking over Asia, while Siyue's method of travel was internal, seeking to expand her own limits.

By the start of her third year at CCTV, Siyue was starting to feel suffocated. She was no longer learning so many new things, and she felt slowed down by the many-layered hierarchy of the state enterprise. Xav urged her to explore her ambitions, and encouraged her to leave CCTV.

In late 2011, Siyue finally left her job. She wanted to be her own boss again, and she wanted to go back to teaching.

———

A few months after she left CCTV, a former colleague asked Siyue if she might be up for joining their delegation to the London Olympics in summer 2012 as an interpreter. Siyue had never been to the UK before and wanted to travel; she said yes, and put in her visa application. But CCTV then changed its line-up for the Olympics and no longer needed Siyue. By then her visa had been approved, and she decided not to waste it.

Siyue landed in London in the late summer. Her first impression was that everyone was very helpful. Just after landing, she got completely confused by the signs at Euston Station and missed her train to Manchester. She went to board the next train, not knowing that unlike China, the UK had privatised its train system, and tickets were only valid for certain train companies and certain lines. The inspector at the gate stopped her. 'I'm so sorry, this is my first day in the UK,' Siyue replied. 'Your first day?' the inspector replied. 'Welcome!' – and let her through. At this point she realised she'd left her phone in the public toilets at the station.

Staying with friends of Xav's in Manchester and London, Siyue also discovered the British concept of class, being told which neighbourhoods were working class, which were middle class, and what those labels meant. 'Don't middle-class people work?' she asked. Xav's friend tried to parse these new concepts for her in ways that added confusion: 'Lots of people say they're working class, but really, in terms of their lifestyles, they're more middle class.'

She understood these labels as describing attitudes: middle-class people expected their children to go to university, for example. She thought these attitudes were more fixed than in the China of her childhood, where village children could grow up wanting to go to university.

Siyue visited Cambridge because it felt like a natural choice for a Chinese tourist. The city had been immortalised in Chinese culture by the poet Xu Zhimo, who was a visiting scholar in the 1920s:

Softly I am leaving,
Just as softly as I came;
I softly wave goodbye
To the clouds in the western sky . . .

The green tape grass rooted in the soft mud
Sways leisurely in the water;

I am willing to be such a waterweed
In the gentle flow of the River Cam . . .

To seek a dream? Go punting with a long pole,
Upstream to where green grass is greener,
With the punt laden with starlight,
And sing out loud in its radiance . . .

One August evening, Siyue floated along the Cam in a shallow wooden punt, the golden light of the setting sun illuminating the stone facades of the colleges and their long lawns. The scene reminded her of the green waterways of her home town, the river where her mother had once asked her if she had wanted to die – a home town made more beautiful in hindsight by her distance from the struggles of her childhood. At that moment, she made a promise to herself: she would find a way to come back every summer.

———

Back in Beijing, one of Xav's friends, a British teacher in his mid-twenties called Benji, was also thinking of ways to become his own boss. Benji had landed in Beijing in the mid-2000s and stayed because he loved the energy of the place: everything was on the up. After a few years in various English-teaching jobs, he had become a part-time teacher at one of the big international schools that had been set up in Beijing's rich north-eastern suburbs.

In the early 2010s, Benji had seen the exploding number of wealthy parents wanting to get their children out of the Chinese school system. He kept coming across parents who wanted to throw money at him in order to get their kids into his school – kids who often barely spoke a word of English, or seemed completely apathetic about studying. There must be a better path for these children, Benji thought. His school was sending him a constant supply of kids for private tuition, but he didn't think that was the best way of helping them. He started talking to Xav about setting up a company that could cater for rich kids who didn't fit into the school system. There was money in it, for sure.

By then in China's big cities, private tuition had become the norm for anyone who could afford it. The middle-class approach to parenting was captured by the stereotype of the 'Haidian mama', named after the north-western district of Beijing that is home to the country's top universities and most intense high schools. One news outlet published snippets of such mothers' diaries under the headline: 'Haidian Mama: My Child Hasn't Wasted One Day Since First Grade.'

Competition starts early, partly because a misallocation of educational resources means the quality of schooling can vary dramatically even in one city. Oversubscribed primary schools demand a list of the child's accomplishments over the six years of their life, and an interview with the parents. The fourteen-page CV of a five-year-old in Shanghai went viral, claiming achievements such as 'reading over 500 English books a year'.

Benji and Xav had been discussing various business ideas for a few months without settling on anything when Xav invited Siyue along to one of their meetings, thinking she would be good at coming up with a plan. Afterwards, Siyue approached her former colleagues at CCTV, her former students' parents, and all of her friends with school-age children, asking what they thought she, Xav and Benji could offer.

By the late 2010s, China had become the world's biggest source of international students. There was an aura of mystery and privilege around the ways students studied and socialised overseas, and a foreign brand-name university would propel you up the social ladder when job hunting back in China. At the same time, international tourism was becoming incredibly attractive to parents, who wanted their children to see the sights they had never been able to see in their own childhoods. Benji, Xav and Siyue decided to test the waters with a summer camp for Chinese primary-school pupils in the Sussex countryside.

Benji had wanted to wait before launching the idea, to design proper brochures and a company website, but Siyue went right back to her CCTV colleagues and recruited six primary-school students straight away. She knew that in China's business world, the most important thing was to satisfy your customers' desires as quickly as possible. Benji arranged spaces at a summer camp held by a British partner company. The camp was a mixture of nationalities: kids from across Europe learning English, British kids learning French, and Siyue's small cohort of six Beijingers, whom she accompanied.

Siyue sat in on their classes, taking notes on the methods of British teachers; she went with them on their afternoon walks along the wheat fields of the southern English countryside; she swayed with them in the evening school discos; she toasted marshmallows with them by the bonfires they built at night. She sometimes wondered if she was having even more fun than the kids. In the guise of being a teacher, Siyue relived a school life as she would have liked it, though the after-school activities were not the kind a Haidian mama would put on her son's CV.

What struck Siyue the most about the British teachers was that they made engaging the kids their main priority: everything, including getting a class to be quiet, could be turned into a game. Most importantly, the teachers engaged with the bad students as much as the good ones.

With the formal English teaching taken care of by their British partner, Will, Siyue was free to assume a more caring role for the kids under her watch. It was the first time she had been responsible purely for her students' non-academic skills. Away from their strict regimens in Beijing, many behavioural oddities emerged among the kids, from severe homesickness to extreme mischief-making.

On Siyue's birthday, Will took her to Cambridge and showed her around the colleges. He asked if she might be interested in holding the camp again in Cambridge.

Siyue didn't hesitate. 'Yes. I'll bring the students.'

———

The first year of Siyue's attempt to set up an education company for international school entry, offering summer camps abroad and tuition in Beijing, was a tangle of emotions. Small disputes with her boyfriend Xav over what to do became big conflicts over working styles, and these arguments left Siyue feeling more and more exhausted.

Xav and Siyue moved from the apartment they had shared in Sanlitun, the dense and lively nightlife district of Beijing, to an apartment in the rich north-eastern suburbs, in order to live near the international schools whose students they were trying to recruit. Xav hated living in the quiet suburbs, and became increasingly unhappy. Siyue was now putting her all into the start-up, but Xav didn't like her taking client calls in the middle of a weekend with him.

'Can you stop it with the continuous self-improvement, and just relax?' he snapped at her, after she got up early one morning to go to the gym. Siyue and Xav started sleeping facing in different directions.

Finally, Siyue told Xav she couldn't keep on going with the start-up if he was also part of it. At the beginning of 2014, Xav left the team. At the end of the year, they broke up.

In retrospect, Siyue wondered if her boyfriends had had an element of the saviour complex. They were incredibly loving when she was lacking in confidence and uncertain of her path, as she had been when trying to improve her English at the scam private college, or setting out on a career at the state television broadcaster. But towards the end of their relationships, as she became more ambitious, they started to sour.

———

For the first time in more than ten years, Siyue didn't have a boyfriend, which meant she had more time on her hands. She started trying out new things with her female friends, like art and Spanish classes.

Siyue's Spanish teacher took her to salsa classes run by a charismatic teacher named Hongyi. Hongyi was an extremely natural performer who wore flats and leggings instead of heels and dresses. She made every move look relaxed and easy. As soon as she finished her demonstration, she would leave the stage and walk among the rows of students, dancing next to them and correcting their steps. Siyue liked Hongyi's student-centric teaching style and told her so.

After a few lessons, Hongyi told Siyue that if she wanted to study salsa properly, she'd need to practise in front of a floor-length mirror, and she had a spare one she could gift her. When Siyue went up to Hongyi's flat to pick it up, they started chatting about their parents. Hongyi's mother was an expert in inflicting verbal wounds, a habit that reminded Siyue of her own parents. These childhood pains had compelled Hongyi to become independent as soon as she could. She had moved to Beijing, where she had taught herself to dance salsa.

Siyue left Hongyi's flat feeling much closer to her. During the next Spring Festival holiday, when everyone else went home to their families, Siyue stayed over at Hongyi's for the week. They decided they would make good flatmates.

They eventually moved into a new flat with Siyue's friend Fanghui. Siyue had met Fanghui, who had also previously started a business, through one of her colleagues from the Olympics English teaching camps. When Siyue was initially trying to start a company with Benji and Xav, she happened to be walking past Fanghui's neighbourhood, and decided to give her a call to ask about her own venture.

That day, Fanghui invited Siyue up to her apartment, and they talked until 2 a.m. She was in the middle of divorcing her husband, and in her description of him, Siyue recognised her own father; she told Fanghui about her own family's arguments and that she supported her decision to leave.

Siyue had a puppy-like curiosity for the women she befriended, especially for those in whom she sensed strength and independence. She was guided by that sense and found it easy to trust her new friends. Hongyi and Fanghui reminded her of her dorm-mates at the private college who always had her back. In the company of the women in her life, she felt secure: you could give your heart away, and they would always hold it for you.

———

Benji and Siyue kept going with the business. Siyue registered the company in Beijing, and recruited thirty students for the next year's Cambridge summer school. Benji continued to work with students seeking entry to international schools. The two of them had an established routine: Siyue, the Chinese-speaking sales face of the company, would sit down with the parents in one room of Benji's apartment, while Benji would take the child into another and play games in English to get to know them. Half an hour later, the two would confer in the corridor to discuss the child's chances; Siyue would then guide the parents' expectations.

Siyue was a natural saleswoman. She could simultaneously empathise with the parents' anxieties and soothe them with her confidence. She believed in what she was selling. She had no front, and none of the elite-school arrogance that sometimes got parents' backs up. In their first two years of running the company, Siyue signed up everyone who visited their makeshift offices: eighty parents in total.

In their business plans, Siyue and Benji referred to the parents as Beijing's 'high net worth individuals'. Generally, these households spent Rmb2 million a year on education for their only children. One thrust Rmb100,000 into Benji's hands as a small thank-you for getting her kid to start paying attention in school. Many of them were entrepreneurs who had, like Siyue's parents, gone 'into the sea' in the early decades of Reform and Opening Up – but, unlike Siyue's parents, had made the kind of money that kept growing of its own accord.

Most of the parents hadn't gone to university themselves – some hadn't completed high school – and barely any of them spoke a word of English. But they all wanted to get their children into English-speaking schools. Siyue and Benji were taken aback by the high sums they could demand from the parents, but at the same time they thought the parents were getting an amazing deal.

Siyue and Benji often felt like they were the first adults who really got to know these over-privileged and under-appreciated children. Although they weren't 'left behind' in the traditional sense of migrant workers' children left in the countryside, their parents were absent in other ways, and often treated their kids with a hard-edged criticism that was undershot with anxiety.

Benji was used to this type of parent from his time as a teacher at the international school. He recalled the parent–teacher meetings in which parents would – before they had even sat down – ask what the problem was with their child. If Benji told them their child was doing well, they would sit impassively while Benji described the child's achievements. When he finished praising them, they would look Benji in the eye and ask again, 'So, what needs improving?' Benji might mention something he thought was a relatively minor concern – 'Oh, they could be more careful about their grammar' – and the parent would start writing down every word. He knew that later that evening his wonderful student was going to get yelled at for their grammar.

This generation of rich parents had risen up through a brutally competitive business world. They knew their children would face even tougher competition in school than they had faced, and would find it difficult to repeat the same economic success they had. They were especially fearful of them 'falling off the ladder' of society, as Siyue put it. And the ladder was growing very tall: the distance from a villa in the suburbs of Beijing to a migrant workers' dormitory in an underground bunker.

At the same time, the parents were highly confident in the power of money to buy anything they wanted, be it a business contract, a regulatory permit, or a prestigious education. *Making the money was the hard part; now you just need to get my child into Harvard.*

Benji and Siyue believed it was the other way round: raising children was the hard part. Many kids that came to them had little intrinsic motivation and had spent their childhoods being ferried from one private tuition class to another. They didn't know where to start when posed with a British private-school entrance exam question like 'Describe your best day' or 'Where would you most like to live in the future?' Many were shy, anxious and afraid of doing anything wrong. And, of course, there were kids they suspected of having undiagnosed problems, such as ADHD or autism spectrum disorder.

Siyue had started to pivot away from traditional language teaching and towards what she considered to be a holistic approach to education, including coaching the parents. In her own schooldays, she had felt the same paralysis that failing students feel when given too much adult pressure. She kept repeating to parents: *If you're in a state of fear, you can't take anything in. You have to solve the problem of fear before you solve anything else. Otherwise, all the extra classes you're paying for are for nothing.*

———

In 2015, Siyue and Benji opened a 'learning centre' in Beijing. In addition to their part-time students, they had now accumulated a few full-time students. These students' parents had taken them out of their former schools for Siyue's teachers to tutor them privately in preparation for international school entry. Siyue and Benji rented a space north-east of the city centre, in a rich suburb near Beijing Capital Airport filled with European-style villas, multinational executives on expat packages – and, most importantly, international schools.

By this point, the company had expanded to employ almost twenty full-time staff members. Their foreign teachers had grown up in various English-speaking countries, under different education systems, but were united by the belief that many education systems were designed completely arbitrarily and could be improved.

Siyue hired her first head of education in 2016 and told her: 'We want to build a new kind of school.' Their mission was to reconnect each student with their innate sense of curiosity. They decided they needed to start from scratch with a new curriculum.

Together, Siyue and her staff came up with the idea of a 'tree' approach to learning based on the Dewey Decimal System, the classification libraries use to organise all human learning. Each branch of the tree was taken from the categories under the system: language, literature, science, and so on. At the start of their course of study, each student would select a few questions within each category that they wanted to spend the next month or two answering. The teachers and students would co-design a curriculum that helped the students research their interests. At the end of the term, all the kids would present their projects, giving them a sense of both responsibility and accountability.

This off-road style of learning meant that occasionally students' projects would fail. But more commonly, left to their own imaginations and individualised instruction, the students would create projects more intricate and in-depth than their parents had ever thought them capable of. At the end of the two months, one fourteen-year-old girl presented a comparative study of Machiavelli and Sun Tzu; one thirteen-year-old boy, who had arrived at the school angry and disengaged, scripted a sharia law trial. Another boy, who had wanted to drop out of school, designed a board game that explained why island ecosystems were so fragile. Another boy presented a very serious talk on taboo language and swearing (which had to be held behind closed doors).

For the parents, who had spent their lives believing that the point of education was to score high grades, it could be difficult at first to allow their kids to focus on growing their curiosity. Siyue's job was to convince them that this experiment in playful learning was vital for removing the psychological blocks their children had developed.

Siyue's school was the kind that she herself wished she could have attended. Instead, she had become a casualty of the dysfunction inherent in the traditional education system. She realised she had dropped out in order to make something better.

———

As the learning centre grew to accommodate more students, Siyue and Benji rented more space in the floors above theirs until the company could no longer be contained there. At the end of 2018, the company moved into a new building that was designed by an architect friend of Siyue's to feel warm and welcoming. It had a theatre space where kids could present their projects, an art room and even a science lab. There was a row of small classrooms for the one-on-one tutoring sessions that took up about half of the students' time. At the heart of the building was a library, where Siyue hoped her students could feel as safe as she had as a child in her grandmother's village home, buried in her aunt's novels.

The company obtained an official licence from the Education Ministry to provide private academic tuition. Although the private tutoring industry was lightly regulated, licences were important to help distinguish real schools from scams – of which there were many.

Business was booming, and rivals were circling. Siyue and Benji were caught in the cut-throat competition for children's time. As a result, they grew used to seeing their students poached by other tutoring companies. Sometimes they would make progress with a kid, gradually developing his confidence, only for his mother to sign him up for the exam-cramming centre down the road. Now that her son was 'fixed', he had to get back to test prep.

It was sad for Siyue and Benji to see students disappear into cram schools, but they knew that they had little control over what happened outside of their school.

12

Should we jump?
Leiya

In 2013, Leiya's daughter Xinling turned five years old. She was a year away from entering primary school. But Leiya needed to get her into one first.

This was a problem of two parts. First, her daughter didn't exist on paper, or at least on the pieces of paper the school needed to register her. Second, even if Xinling had existed legally, she would have had a *hukou* household registration in the village Leiya had run away from at the age of fifteen – not in Shenzhen, the city where she lived.

Leiya saw some hope for solving the second problem. In the early 2010s, some cities began to slightly relax their *hukou* requirements to admit some migrant workers' children. They adopted a points-based system, whereby migrant children could get into a city school if their parents accumulated enough points through their own educational achievements and model-citizen behaviour.

Leiya started keeping track of the long tables of point-awarding criteria, with an eye towards getting Xinling accepted to a city school. Chufeng, by now her husband, didn't see why she was going to so much trouble: he thought it would be fine for Xinling to live with her grandmother back in his old village. 'That's what all the other families are doing, and their kids manage to survive,' Chufeng would say.

Leiya disagreed, but she knew Chufeng's point of view was also the government's. The cities wanted rural workers to fuel their factories, but they were only wanted as labour, not as humans. Leiya and her fellow workers were expected to go back to their ancestral villages for health care, for retirement, and for their children's education. For them, the city was a place of labour, not of living.

But Leiya didn't see things this way: she belonged to the city now, and she wanted her daughter to belong, too. Chufeng didn't know what it would be like for Xinling to become a left-behind child. Unlike Leiya, he had never experienced the cold of an empty home. Leiya was determined to keep Xinling in the city. *Aiya*, it was always the mothers who had to do everything, she told herself with a sigh.

Points for school entry were awarded for technical certifications like the computer course Leiya had taken, and for her qualification as a labour dispute mediator, which she had obtained at the City Workers' Community Centre, before she left to set up the Garland District Women's Centre.

In addition to accumulating points, migrants also needed years of records documenting their legal residence and social insurance payments. Luckily, Leiya's community work had involved giving advice to migrant workers on the social insurance system, and she had started paying her own insurance contributions long in advance of her daughter going to school, with the aim of establishing a good payment record.

But Leiya soon realised that her efforts to gain points for school entry might amount to nothing. Since Xinling had been born outside marriage, her birth was a violation of the population-control policy. By the mid-2010s, government figures suggested there were 13 million people without any kind of *hukou*, of whom 8 million had been children outside their parents' birth quotas. Although by law these children were technically allowed to register for *hukou* without barriers, in practice, local authorities routinely charged high fees or gated access to services for such children.

Leiya could have paid extra for a place at a privately run school that served migrants' children, but she didn't trust them. They popped up and then disappeared, and often the teachers didn't have any teaching qualifications at all. Leiya firmly set her sights on the state school just on the edge of her urban settlement.

Thus began six months of exhausting her options. First, Leiya tried getting the date on her marriage certificate officially 'corrected' to an earlier date. She temporarily left her job in order to travel thousands of miles to her old home town. She filled in piles of paperwork to make her own status look more respectable, obtaining a little government-issued booklet that verified her as a *member of the mobile population*. She gifted cigarettes to local government clerks. She called in favours. She begged and pleaded. She told plenty of white lies to any officials who would listen. But this didn't amount to anything.

Months later, back in her tiny flat in the urban village, Leiya decided it was time for the big lie. If she was caught, Leiya thought, there was a chance that her daughter wouldn't be able to go to school. But if she didn't even try, that outcome was certain.

Leiya picked up a pencil. She pressed it firmly onto the dateline of her marriage certificate, drawing a thick numeral that obscured what had been written underneath. In those few seconds, she lengthened her marriage by a year.

Now, the certificate said that she had been a bride at the age of twenty-one – and consequently had been married before Xinling's birth. After she photocopied the certificate, the change was barely noticeable. Her five-year-old daughter was one step closer to school.

———

It was unsettlingly easy to forge documents, at least back then, before the days of digital records and microchips in ID cards. On the walls of the urban settlement were graffiti adverts for agents promising anyone a new ID card. All through the 2010s, at the gates of labour exchanges, merchants would try to sell everything from falsified graduation certificates to ID cards for underage workers.

The big lie was only one part of Leiya's overall plan. In addition to the marriage and birth certificates, Leiya gathered together her tax and social insurance payment records, her and Chufeng's educational attainment histories, and her residence permit.

Then Leiya turned her focus back to tallying their family's points. The number of points one needed to secure a child's place in school varied year to year, depending on the level of competition from other parents. Leiya was aiming for at least 300 points.

Although she hadn't graduated from middle school, Leiya had completed an adult education high-school course, which earned her 20 points. Chufeng had finished vocational college, which was worth 35 points. (If either of them had obtained an undergraduate degree, it would've brought them 50 points.) Leiya received another 30 points for being under thirty years of age – young migrants were more desirable in the eyes of the city.

The other major point categories were out of reach: Leiya had never founded a profit-making company, applied to register a patent, or worked for a high-tech enterprise. Her income was far too low for her tax contributions to earn points. She had never received an Award of Excellence from the Central Communist Party or the provincial government. She had never been officially recognised as a Good Person of the Community by the city government. After seven years at the community centre, she had helped hundreds of migrant workers solve their workplace disputes. But since she was not working for the government, her work was at best ignored by the authorities, and at worst regarded with suspicion.

At the end of the official point-scoring list, there were smaller rewards and deductions for good or bad behaviour. Every hour's shift working as an Outstanding City Volunteer for the local council would earn Leiya one additional point; blood donations were worth two points. These were little measures she could take to improve her chances of competing with the better-educated migrant parents in her area.

Thankfully, Leiya had no deductions. She had never been marked as being untrustworthy in the local government credit database for selling poor-quality goods or owing money. She had never evaded her taxes. She had no criminal charges.

Still, Leiya was anxious about relying too heavily on the points-based system. Her backup plan was to buy an apartment in the catchment area of the local primary school, which would get her a guaranteed place. Leiya had worked out that the cost would be about the same as going through the points-based system.

Although by law schools in China cannot charge for compulsory education for children aged six to fifteen, they levy all sorts of other fees to raise money. For the children of migrant workers, state schools used to charge a 'temporary study fee'; after this policy was cancelled in 2010, some schools continued charging migrants under the guise of a 'school assistance fee'. Over six years of primary school, Leiya's fees would have totaled over Rmb100,000: the majority of what a factory worker could earn within the same time frame. Rmb100,000 was about the same as the cost of a down payment on a tiny flat in the urban settlement behind the school, which could guarantee Xinling a place and also exempt her from the school assistance fees. Either way, Leiya reasoned, she'd have to spend the money. She bought the flat and moved her family in.

―――

Leiya's points accrual was ultimately the deciding factor in securing Xinling a spot in the local primary school. In a twist of fate, the local school changed its catchment area a few months before Xinling was due to start school, meaning the family's new flat no longer guaranteed her admission.

But as soon as Leiya conquered one adversary – the *hukou*-based school entrance system – another emerged. Towards the end of 2013, the factories in her region of the Pearl River Delta began to relocate further inland, into the western provinces of Sichuan and Chongqing, where labour was cheaper. Some left China entirely for south east Asia.

Many of these companies' competitive advantage in producing exports had come from low wages rather than gains in productivity or technology. But by the 2010s, the supply of rural workers who were willing to work for next to nothing was drying up. The young workforce was shrinking.

To attract more workers, companies had to raise wages or move elsewhere.

For Leiya and the Garland District Women's Centre, the wave of factory relocations meant a fresh onslaught of problems to solve for workers whose factories downsized or disappeared, along with months of owed wages. In the worst cases, workers who had spent decades at one plant without being paid the social insurance they were owed were abandoned without pensions. Although companies have been legally required to pay insurance since the 1990s, coverage for migrant workers remains insufficient to this day.

The first generation of female migrant workers was now nearing the state retirement age of fifty. But none of the 100,000 women workers in Leiya's Garland District neighbourhood had social insurance, meaning they had no city pensions. Women in their forties started coming to Leiya for advice. Some wanted to go back to their villages to care for new-born grandchildren; others wanted to stay in the city but didn't know how they could afford to do so. One of these women, an electronics assembly worker named Guihua, made a strong impression on Leiya with her disarming way of saying whatever was on her mind.

'I don't want to go back home,' Guihua said. 'Going home would be like falling into a 10,000-foot abyss.'

Leiya understood the urge to grip the city tightly; despite the gruelling factory work that had defined her entry to the city in her late teens, Shenzhen remained a haven from the countryside. Leiya associated her childhood in the village with small-minded bullying, the social misery of families with too many daughters, and the pettiness of little places. Once you had experienced the openness and expansiveness of the city, how could you ever go back?

The women who came to see Leiya began talking to one another. They identified their common fear: reaching retirement age, or getting laid off, before their companies had paid the minimum number of years of social insurance for their pensions. It was time to organise.

———

Guihua became one of the core organisers at her audio electronics factory in the Garland District, which manufactured Sony speakers and Apple earbuds. Of 10,000 workers in the factory, over 99 per cent were women. In the autumn of 2013, the workers began to petition the factory management to pay the social insurance that had never gone into their accounts.

Guihua and her fellow organisers would often skip lunch or dinner to distribute leaflets among their colleagues, urging them to sign their petition. The organisers would meet in the evenings to plan the next day's activities, rotating around various venues near the factory: the food court in the basement of the shopping mall, the public square, the streets of the urban village nearby. They knew the factory was sending informants to spy on their meetings, so they had to change venues often. After a few months, 1,500 of the factory's 10,000 workers had signed the petition.

Initially, the group was led by the most persuasive personalities. But soon they decided they needed a more formal leadership structure. The factory lacked an official union and wouldn't respond to the group's calls to create one. Undeterred, the women went ahead themselves. They elected a workers' representative to present their petition to the management, a woman who Guihua admired for her ability to strike at the heart of an argument with one remark, like a nurse finding the right vein from which to draw blood.

The factory's response was to call the local police to arrest the representative. But detaining one worker for a few days did nothing but anger the many other workers who supported the petition. The makeshift union persisted in its attempts to negotiate with management. After all, they reasoned, the factory couldn't call the police to arrest a tenth of their entire staff. By the end of the year, the factory agreed to pay, with two important caveats: the social insurance repayments would only cover the past ten years of each worker's employment, and they would take several years to administer.

The workers were divided. The younger ones who had started work in the 2000s wanted to accept the offer, while the older ones who were on the verge of retirement wanted to hold out for more. Ten years of insurance payments meant they would still be five years short of qualifying for the state pension. At the same time, the factory started restricting the workers' opportunities to organise by limiting toilet breaks and the time they had to meet each other outside the factory floor. A few months later, they started firing the main activists one by one, until they had eliminated some sixty of the most vocal union organisers.

Although Guihua had narrowly escaped the firings, she was now blacklisted by the factory, which meant greater scrutiny from management and no chance of promotion. But she understood that if she backed down now, she would lose her only chance of retiring in the Garland District, where she had spent the best part of her working years. She persevered.

The threat of being fired made Guihua and the other remaining organisers decide they needed to register themselves as an official trade union, so that their representatives would receive some legal protection. The women sought guidance on union law from Leiya, who in turn rapidly taught herself about the topic with the help of friendly labour lawyers. The law was the only thing the women had on their side, so they had to learn to use it.

Guihua and her fellow organisers went to the local branch of the All-China Federation of Trade Unions, the government body which oversees all unions. The branch refused the women's application to form a union, then presented them with a model constitution for a trade union and told them to copy it out by hand. The workers didn't know how to read and write such formal Chinese; Leiya had always explained the law to them in plain language.

After a few weeks of puzzling through the government document, Guihua and her colleagues managed to finalise their application and went back to the branch office. But it was too late. The staff told them that the factory management had called earlier that day and trumped them by registering their own union first. 'You should join their union instead,' the staff advised, 'or your relationship with the factory will only deteriorate.'

Incensed and afraid, the organisers threw their efforts into overdrive. So did the factory management, who continued to fire prominent activists and subject the remaining organisers to increased surveillance, even installing cameras at their workstations. The activists were suspicious of the official factory union's offers to help, but decided to test it by raising smaller issues, such as reducing the length of their eleven-hour shifts. After the union did nothing but make excuses, Guihua's suspicions were confirmed: as she put it, the factory management and the union were wearing the same pair of trousers.

The workers appealed to the higher-level branches of the ACFTU to no avail, and so they decided to turn to the city's

Social Security Bureau. The factory was obliged to pay this bureau, they reasoned, so it might be able to intervene in their case. Guihua and her colleagues staged a day-long protest, sitting in the courtyard of the bureau in the stifling July heat. Every day the women spent organising meant another day of lost wages and being one step closer to being fired.

Just before the bureau closed at 5 p.m., the director finally agreed to take down the workers' names and look into the issue. The women remained sat down. A few hours after nightfall, factory management arrived on the scene and promised a lump-sum repayment of social security to any workers who agreed to resign.

No, Guihua and her colleagues said, they wanted everyone to receive the funds they were owed from the date they started working. The factory said that that was impossible, as they had lost their payroll records from the 1990s.

A week later, the Social Security Bureau staff visited the factory and ordered it to pay every worker a lump sum of social insurance for the past decade, effectively forcing them to accept the factory's original offer. Crucially, it meant that older workers on the verge of turning fifty would soon retire without a pension and have to leave the city – to fall into the abyss.

In a fit of desperation, Guihua's friend shouted at the head of human resources, 'So what do we do now? Should we jump from the roof, like the Geshibi shoe factory staff?' – referencing a recent incident in which a striking female worker had killed herself. Several of her fellow workers yelled out in support of her intervention.

The HR head, not missing a beat, replied calmly that killing themselves wouldn't entitle their families to much compensation. 'After the Foxconn workers realised they wouldn't get much money out of it, they stopped jumping, too.'

Although the factory's settlement didn't address the problems of the older women on the cusp of retirement, it did grant social security to almost 10,000 workers who had previously not been covered: a significant victory. Guihua still feels proud of the number of women who joined the cause – not just from her own factory, but from the surrounding factories as well.

The news spread quickly. *Did you hear about the twenty women who threatened to jump off their factory roof and got everyone social insurance?* Soon, women workers from other factories were demanding social insurance. Some factories even paid their workers before any protests began in order to stave off disruptions to production. At times it felt to Guihua as if the whole of the Garland District had caught fire with the heat of organising – a fire that she had had some part in lighting.

Yet Guihua's victory came too late to help her personally. An unexpected national-level policy change meant that she, like other migrant workers whose factories did not pay their contributions until late into their working lives, was no longer eligible for a state pension in her city.

Her own factory refused to keep her on past the retirement age; she suspected they were cautious about retaining someone who had been a core troublemaker. So after she left, she took jobs paying by the day at different factories around the Garland District, for about Rmb14 an hour. She found day-rate work exhausting, because it meant switching around locations, doing different things all the time; at her age, Guihua would prefer to have a stable job. Like the one she had before.

After working for twenty years in the electronics factory, and despite all of her fights with the management, Guihua is so used to the warehouses and routines that to her it feels like home. On warm evenings, when she walks by the factory gates, she feels the pull of her feet wanting to repeat their old steps. All she wants to do is to walk through the gates and keep on working.

———

After the protests came the crackdown. Leiya had expected this; she reasoned that the government was also responsible for contributing some of the social insurance payments, and likely didn't want the outlay. In the mid-2010s, the government started seeing labour organising as a political threat that needed to be systematically confronted. But she still stood by the women workers. To switch sides was unthinkable to Leiya, whose teen years had been marked by management's abuses of power, and who empathised with the women's desire to hold on to the city in their retirement.

First, the local authorities started driving the labour NGOs out of their rented offices. Leiya received a sudden call from her landlord saying he wasn't renewing their contract. He gave no reason, and just said that she'd better go somewhere else. This became a common experience for other labour NGO leaders, who were continually forced to move from block to block. Once they were pushed out of the district, they would be another police force's problem.

Finally, the police started arresting people.

———

Leiya was pulled in for questioning a few times, but she escaped relatively unscathed. She could continue her work of supporting women workers so long as she was careful how she advertised her events, and which issues she took on. Ultimately, it wasn't the government's harassment that forced her to wind down her operations in the Garland District, but the demands of motherhood.

Xinling was about to start going to the state-run primary school that stood on the edge of Lion's Head Village, the urban settlement where Leiya had originally bought her apartment in the hope of securing her daughter a school place. While the Garland District was dominated by vast, uniform apartment blocks and wide roads that wound around factory campuses, the Lion's Head Village was much denser and consisted of illegally erected buildings erratically tacked onto one another. Most Lion's Head Village families lived in ten-metre-square flats with one bedroom and a kitchen.

Leiya now had to find childcare for her daughter in the few hours between school ending at 4 p.m. and she and her husband returning from work. Xinling was too old to go to the private kindergarten nearby, and Leiya couldn't afford a nanny.

After years of experience in community organising, Leiya understood her conundrum as a social issue. *I'm not the only one in this situation*, she thought. *There must be plenty of other mothers like me, many working even longer hours.* She knew she would eventually be forced by the government to shut down her women's centre in the Garland District, so she decided to open a new one in Lion's Head Village, a place where mothers could take turns looking after each other's children.

Leiya struck up conversations with the other mothers in the area, asking them how they managed their childcare. Many had sent their children to live with the grandparents in their rural home towns. Some kept their children in the city and locked them in their flats while they were gone. Leiya thought this unsafe: in such cramped flats, with loose electrical wiring all over the walls and taps dripping into open drains, it would be easy for an accident to happen. Next, Leiya handed out surveys to assess working mothers' needs, gathering evidence that there was demand for a children's centre.

All of this work ran over the summer of 2015 and spilled into her daughter's first term at school. Leiya's mother had returned to their home village for a short stint, and as much as it pained her, Leiya sent Xinling to stay with her while she continued making preparations for the centre. 'You're going to the countryside for a little while, but it's all in order to have a better future,' she kept telling the six-year-old Xinling in the run-up to her departure.

To her relief, Xinling was only gone for a few months. Halfway through the autumn term, Leiya had secured enough funding from local mothers and other donors to rent a spacious hundred-square-metre apartment on the first floor of a building in Lion's Head Village, for Rmb1,200 per month.

When Leiya opened the centre, she told the kids to drag in their plastic desks from home so they could do their homework after school. In the summers, she asked them to bring their own electric fans to beat away the soporific humidity. The mothers took turns to open up the centre at the end of the school day.

———

In 2015, when Xinling was due to start primary school, a series of deaths drew the nation's attention to the plight of left-behind children. In Guizhou province, four siblings aged five to thirteen killed themselves by drinking pesticide. In Hunan province, two girls were poisoned by a classmate.

All of them were left-behind children. In the early 2010s, over 60 million Chinese children – one in five – lived without their parents. One in fourteen lived alone. Initiatives like Leiya's children's centre were praised by local charities, and begrudgingly accepted by the local authorities, for making it possible for children to stay with their parents.

A tight-knit community of mothers formed around the centre, and everyone chipped in to buy permanent desks and fans. Some supporters donated benches. One of the larger charitable foundations in Guangdong province even gave them one year's rent; Leiya was elated that the centre might have some staying power. Eventually, the local Civil Affairs Bureau caught wind of Leiya's project and called to ask her to officially register the centre with the local government.

Looking back, Leiya knows she would never have tried to start the centre if she'd foreseen all the obstacles she'd meet later on. To formally register the centre, she needed to raise more capital, as well as to meet the onerous fire-safety requirements, which police and fire brigades across China often use to extract bribes. After much effort, Leiya eventually submitted her application for the 'Working Parents' Community Care Centre'.

Her request was initially rejected because the word 'working' – *dagong*, the term for low-skilled labour – was flagged as politically sensitive. So Leiya came up with a new name: the Banyan Tree Centre. Banyans are common in southern China, and their vast root systems hang from their branches, stretching for metres through the air and extending far beneath the earth. Leiya wanted to evoke a sense of rootedness in the community, hoping that the centre would continue to grow long into the future. She printed the name on a canvas banner and hung it above the centre's now-official entrance, offering its welcome to all the families nearby.

13

Breaking the cycle
Siyue

Thanks to the success of her education company, Siyue finally had a thick cushion of savings, and she decided to spend it taking her mother, Sulan, on holiday. She wanted to show Sulan how large and beautiful the world could be, but most of all, she wanted to kindle a mother–daughter relationship based on mutual enjoyment rather than the arguments that had defined her childhood.

Leisure was not a familiar concept to Sulan. Throughout Siyue's childhood, she had seen herself primarily as a mother and provider for the family, earning enough to compensate for Siyue's father's stock-market gambling. Now that Siyue had left home, she saw herself as a grandmother-in-waiting, someone to be called upon to do chores for her extended family. Leisure meant taking short breaks to watch television. She initially rejected Siyue's offers to take her travelling.

Siyue anticipated her mother's resistance, and tricked her into a holiday by claiming she had bought non-refundable flight tickets – she knew that Sulan's desire to avoid wasting money would trump her instinct to stay home. With that, they boarded a plane to Bali.

At first, Sulan complained that they were going to a lot of trouble to visit a place as rural as a Chinese village, but fell quiet one morning when they watched the sunrise over the ocean. Together they went ziplining through a jungle, practised yoga on the beach at sunset and swam in an infinity pool perched at the edge of a cliff. Even if Sulan wouldn't outwardly admit it, Siyue knew the truth: her mother was having fun.

Gradually, Sulan started to change her mind about exploring the world. She even asked Siyue to teach her a few sentences of English so that she could eventually travel on her own. As it turned out, she too had a knack for picking up new ideas. Over time, the fear of scarcity that had been the dominating force in Sulan's life started to lessen.

Siyue also wanted to share some of her emotional and intellectual life with her mother. She recommended her the self-help books she liked – *The Secret* and *The Law of Attraction* – so they would have more to discuss beyond cooking and laundry. (For her grumpy father, she recommended *A Complaint-Free World*.)

Towards the end of 2017, Siyue became pregnant. Her boyfriend at the time left China shortly afterwards, and Siyue knew she would have to raise a child on her own. But at the age of thirty-one, with a successful business to provide for her, Siyue felt ready. She discussed her decision with her female flatmates, who unanimously supported her.

At the start of 2018, when Siyue was five months pregnant, she finally convinced her father Zijian to join her mother on a trip abroad. She signed them up for a tour of Canada which took them to a hot spring in the Rocky Mountains. Her father seemed to relax ever so slightly: he no longer stayed up until 3 a.m. each night to scrutinise the movements of stock prices.

(Though he never bought stocks again after the 2001 crash, he continued trading fantasy stocks.)

When they landed back in Beijing, Zijian stepped off the flight and exclaimed, 'The air here is so bad, my chest hurts already.' Beijing's smog was worst in the winters. But the next day, Zijian was still uncomfortable. Zijian went on his own to the hospital in their home town, while Sulan stayed in Beijing for an extra day: she wanted to knead and wrap enough steamed buns to fill Siyue's freezer. When Sulan arrived at the hospital the following evening to see how Zijian was doing, she found the doctors had already admitted him for inpatient care.

The next morning, the doctors took Sulan aside, out of Zijian's earshot. 'The lung cancer is very serious,' they said. 'You have two options: he can undergo chemotherapy, which will give him another month at most, but will be painful and stressful for him. Or you can take him home.'

Sulan made her mind up on the spot to take Zijian home. If he had less than a month to live, she wanted him to enjoy it. Like most Chinese relatives, she didn't tell him his diagnosis, nor did the doctors – who often help patients' loved ones hide terminal diagnoses from them.

'We're going home,' she told him. 'There's nothing urgent to do. Let's just continue the holiday.'

———

In the wake of her father's death, to Siyue's surprise, Sulan grieved Zijian deeply. In his absence, she seemed to have scrubbed her memory of all the bitter tempers he had carried in his life, leaving only sweet remnants. Whereas before Siyue and Sulan had formed a united front against her father, now Sulan was making excuses for his past behaviour. In death he was blameless.

Siyue was conflicted. One part of her was resentful. She was shocked by the extent to which her mother had unilaterally changed the narrative of their family. She wanted to remind Sulan of how much she had hated her husband at various times. Another part of her was glad to see her mother's love for her father, and to see his good intentions remain in her memory of him.

A third part of Siyue was angry that she had assumed responsibility for her mother's happiness throughout her twenties, striving to buy her mother financial independence from her father. Since Siyue was little, her parents' fiercest fights had been over money; she thought that making a fortune would improve things between them. If, after all these years, her mother hadn't suffered so much, what was the point of all the effort Siyue had put in to protecting her?

Yet another part of her was relieved that she no longer felt the need to be her mother's protector.

With her father gone, Siyue also felt more picked on by her mother; when they were united against her father, Sulan had taken things out on him instead. Now they were more frequently at odds, and Siyue wondered about how her baby's imminent arrival might further change things between them.

Siyue talked through all these feelings with her flatmates, whom she would still eat dinner with most evenings. If she had been living alone, she thought, she would have never been able to get through those times. She had been denied siblings by the one-child policy, but she had found the best of sisters in Beijing.

Just before she was due to give birth, Siyue moved into a larger flat further from the city centre, and Sulan moved in with her. Siyue's former flatmates visited every weekend, often bringing small gifts: a padded mat for the newborn to lie on, a small wooden toy that was light enough for an infant to hold. She was happy that they had selected functional items and well-loved hand-me-downs, rather than flashy, expensive gifts. Between her father's passing, her ever-changing relationship with her mother, and the prospect of being a single working mother, Siyue had had a lot to process during her pregnancy. Having her girlfriends around reassured her that she had the support she needed to survive. She was excited and comforted by the thought that her daughter would grow up in the company of such spectacular women.

———

Ever the autodidact, Siyue prepared herself for parenthood by reading books about infant education. Years before, on behalf of her company, she had taken part in several 'Positive Discipline' training courses geared towards educators working with teenagers. Positive Discipline is a school of thought descended from the psychotherapeutic approach of Alfred Adler, who believed that children developed best under firm, respectful parenting, rather than cycles of reward and punishment that bred resentment and dependency. Siyue took naturally to the idea, thinking back to the family-induced anxiety of her school years.

One of the books that Siyue read during her pregnancy on Positive Discipline for infants had a section that resonated with her:

> What your little one most needs to learn in the first three
> years of life isn't found on flash cards or electronic screens.
> Brain development is all about connection with other
> people, and your child's brain is wired to seek connection
> from the moment of birth. How you and your child's
> other caregivers relate to her – how you talk and play and

nurture – is by far the most important factor in a baby or toddler's development.[1]

Siyue posted the quote on her WeChat social media account, along with a photo of the page on which it appeared, which discussed the philosophy of the early childhood educator Magda Gerber. Within a few hours, her yoga teacher messaged her to ask if she would like to join a WeChat Group of Magda Gerber fans. Gerber was the founder of the Resources for Infant Educarers (RIE) method, which shared many principles with Positive Discipline, but was specifically tailored for infants, with recommendations for everything from bedtime routines to nappy-changing.

Siyue joined, and read the regular updates about RIE training courses and books. She prepared her new flat in RIE fashion: she left the living room almost bare, clearing out anything that might prove a hazard for a crawling baby, so that her daughter would be free to play and explore confidently with minimum interference from her.

The only furniture in Siyue's living room was a sofa, as well as a triangle climbing frame with a slide on one side. This toy is known as a 'Pikler Triangle', named after the Hungarian paediatrician who inspired Madga Gerber. It was the kind of toy Sulan might have thought too dangerous for a toddler, but the RIE philosophy was about learning to trust the child with age-appropriate tasks that encouraged their development. Swaddling them in cloths so thickly that they couldn't move freely, as was customary in some parts of China, prioritised a certain kind of safety at the expense of the development of their gross motor skills. Siyue wanted her child to be free to explore the world, and to be confident in doing so.

[1]Nelsen, Jane, et al., *Positive Discipline: The First Three Years*, Three Rivers Press, 2015

In 2018, a few months after her father's death, Siyue gave birth to her daughter. She decided to name her 'Eva', after 'Evangelina', Greek for 'bearer of good news': she wanted a name that spoke of hope.

Though China had partially relaxed its one-child policy three years earlier, in 2015, many parts of the old population planning system remained. Children born outside marriage were still counted as 'exceeding the birth quota', and the mother was charged a 'social maintenance fee'.

The fees were cancelled in 2021, when Eva was three years old, as part of the government's effort to convince more women to have children, in an attempt to reverse the rapid decline in the working-age population caused by its policies. Mothers like Siyue who had paid the social maintenance fines joked that they should try to get their money back.

Single parents like Siyue were growing in number but uncounted in the official statistics. One academic, Wan Haiyuan, estimated the number of children born outside marriage in the early 2010s at over a million.

Siyue gave birth in a private hospital, as public hospitals wouldn't deliver children being born outside marriage. She managed to pay her Rmb10,000 'social maintenance' fine with her profits from her education company.

A few weeks after she gave birth, Siyue visited the RIE centre in Beijing; four months later, she attended her first course there.

Siyue's biggest task was to prepare Sulan, who would become Eva's caregiver while Siyue was at work, to raise Eva with the RIE guidelines in mind. She knew this would not be an easy process: many parents are hostile when their children suggest new parenting methods to them, seeing this as a criticism of their own methods. Siyue gently explained RIE's core principles to Sulan, which revolve around instilling a sense of security, respect and boundaries.

Respect, for example, was expressed by telling the infant what the adult intended to do before they did it. In RIE workshops, Siyue had participated in an exercise where the adults in the room took a tissue and tried to wipe something from another adult's face as if they were a baby without warning them first. The natural instinct when someone came at your face out of the blue was to flinch; it felt like an attack. Babies can feel that fear, too, the instructor said. So first tell them, 'I'm going to wipe something from your face.' Give them time to react. Then do it.

Sulan's first response was incredulity: what was the point of prefacing one's actions for a tiny infant who doesn't understand words? She told Siyue that she would love Eva with her whole heart, and that would be enough.

'Love and respect aren't the same thing,' Siyue replied. She bought Sulan a Chinese translation of *Baby Knows Best*, a book on the RIE method by the educator Deborah Carlisle Solomon. Sulan initially resisted, saying that she was too old for studying. But Siyue remained firm and continued to demonstrate the RIE approach to Sulan through her actions at home.

The first RIE principle that Siyue put into practice was the idea that children like routine: she woke, fed, bathed and changed nappies for Eva at the same time every day. She observed Eva as she learned to lift her upper body and start crawling around the room, not interfering unless she was in harm's way. She started speaking to Eva as if she were an understanding adult, alerting her before she picked her up or whatever else she was about to do. Sulan watched and, gradually, she became curious.

Sulan began to treat daily chores like nappy-changing as shared rituals and conversations with Eva, making eye contact and explaining the process to the baby throughout. After a couple of months, she noticed subtle changes in the way Eva responded, lifting her bottom slightly when Sulan told her she was about to take off her nappy.

Encouraged by these developments, Sulan grew more confident in Siyue's chosen method. She even felt that this style of parenting relieved her own anxiety, in a way, making her feel more deliberate and assured in her choices. Eva's behaviour seemed calmer and more predictable than that of the other babies in their compound, who were more prone to erratic outbursts.

During the daytime, when parents were at work, Beijing's gardens and parks filled with grandparents and babies, toddlers and preschool children. The grandparents mostly hovered over their grandchildren, not trusting them to do anything on their own. Sulan saw how stressed and burnt-out they were. Friends her age who were tasked with caring for their children's children back home told her they were just gritting their teeth and enduring the first five years until the kids were old enough to go to school. *But what kind of life is that?* Sulan thought. *At this age, even if we can bear it, isn't it bad for our health to be so tense all the time?* Sulan was Eva's only grandparent; she needed to take care of herself, too.

Behind Siyue's desire to have Sulan adopt her parenting style was a deep need to soothe the hurt she had experienced in her own childhood. Long before she gave birth to Eva, she had hoped her tiger mother might renounce her old ways.

But years of close-range sparring had never changed Sulan's mind. Sulan thought that she had done everything in her power to give Siyue the best possible start in life, and just wanted to make sure she did well in school. Everything had been for Siyue's benefit – it was just that Siyue didn't realise it at the time.

Only after Eva was born did Sulan start to consider the complexity of the child's perspective. She had seen Siyue as an extension of herself, as a project to be managed. She had expected total obedience. She was so focused on securing a better life for her daughter that she didn't appreciate Siyue's own experience. By observing Siyue's relationship with Eva, Sulan began to see her daughter's point of view, and reflect on whether, growing up, Siyue had been happy.

———

When Eva was two years old, Sulan took her on her first trip back to her own village. By then, the RIE principles of parenting had become second nature. But she also knew how bizarre her methods would look in the eyes of her siblings and her own mother.

One morning, she decided to pay her respects to a recently bereaved friend who lived far outside the village. Eva was about to have her lunchtime nap, and it wasn't the kind of visit where bringing Eva would have been appropriate. Her sisters urged her to put Eva to bed and quietly slink out of the house before she noticed. By the time she woke up, Sulan would be gone.

This was how it was always done: parents would disappear and children would find themselves alone. If the adults weren't around to witness the tears, it was easier to imagine there weren't any. From the traditional Chinese perspective, talking about an impending separation was pointless: children were dumb, and besides, it never did any good to discuss bad news in advance. Looming departures are hidden from one's children, cancers from one's parents.

When Sulan was a child, it was common for parents to lock their children in the house on their own while the rest of the family went to work in the fields. Though it could be dangerous, families often had little choice in the matter. Little feet were burnt on coal embers. In one particularly tragic incident, a neighbour's baby was killed while left home alone, bitten to death by the pig they were raising.

When Sulan was getting Eva ready for her lunchtime nap that day, she told her: 'Eva, I've got to go out now, so there's a chance that when you wake up, I won't be here. If that's the case, don't worry. You can let any of the aunties in the house put your clothes on for you. Just yell for your aunties.'

Eva looked at her calmly, as if she understood. Sulan's sisters looked at her like she was insane. But when Eva woke up and saw that Sulan was gone, she didn't cry.

———

When Eva was three years old, Siyue gifted Sulan a series of online life-coaching classes, geared towards professional women in Beijing. Sulan didn't like the idea, but she went anyway: Siyue had already made the payment. In their first round of introductions, Sulan told the trainer she was attending to become a better grandmother.

In the end, she got so much out of the course that she recommended it to her own friends. The biggest change she noticed in herself was that she became more confident; she wasn't as prone to helplessness or self-criticism. Previously, in moments of self-doubt, her body would generate a damp anger, a heat that wouldn't disperse. The coach taught her to pause and ask herself certain questions when she felt the heat rising: in short, to coach herself. Sulan liked this practice. She complained to Siyue less and trusted herself more to solve issues on her own. She felt far less anxious, capable of observing instead of immediately responding to the urge to judge and criticise.

By the age of three, Eva was highly verbal and precociously confident. When guests came to visit, she would answer the door with an uncannily adult air, asking them if they wanted something to eat or drink and then fetching it. When Siyue was feeling down, she would tell Eva in the direct manner that RIE encourages: 'Mama's feeling sad today.' Eva would kiss her cheeks and bring her an apple, which she would warm for Siyue by rubbing it between her palms.

Siyue also tried to acknowledge Eva's emotions by observing them and reflecting them back to her: 'I see you're crying; you're feeling sad.' Siyue had a spare room in her flat with nothing but cushions and a mattress on the floor where she would take Eva when she was in the grip of a tantrum: a soft place where she could blow off steam without hurting herself. Siyue would sit quietly with Eva until she calmed again.

'Why am I like this?' Eva once asked. 'Why don't adults get angry and scream?'

'You're a little kid, so there are some things you can't handle yet, like big feelings. Your brain will keep growing until you're twenty-five,' Siyue replied. (And besides, she almost added, some adults *do* get angry and scream.)

Siyue wanted Eva to know that it was okay to feel anger and despair and resentment, but there was a time and place to act out those emotions. Once the tantrum passed, they would leave the room together.

Eva was growing up surrounded by affirmation. Siyue joked with her friends that this would make her a dangerous woman when she was older. *Can you imagine what we would have been like if we had been raised this way?*

———

Sometimes Siyue would feel pessimistic about whether she could ultimately break the cycle of generational trauma; she and Sulan could go backwards as well as forwards. One evening, Siyue came home to find her mother sitting in the living room stony-faced. Sulan recounted that, when she went to pick Eva up from kindergarten, the teacher had told her off in front of all the other parents because Eva had taken so long to put on her shoes and coat at the end of the day.

Sulan had stood there frozen, aware of the many other parents who would have heard the teacher's admonishments. She had walked home in a daze, forgetting to chat or play with Eva. By the time they reached the flat, she had come to a conclusion: Eva must do better. She put her to bed early that evening.

'Eva needs to work on her time management,' Sulan told Siyue. Hearing her mother say this, Siyue's instinct was to leave the room; she was overcome with the feeling of powerlessness she had experienced in her own childhood.

She left the flat, walked down to Benji's a few floors below, and knocked on his door. Benji saw that she was shaking with anger. She sat down on his sofa, and Benji went to get himself a beer.

Siyue was furious with the teacher. 'It was so unfair of her to single Eva out,' she said. After she had ranted for a few minutes and began to calm down, she sighed. 'I don't know why I'm overreacting like this.'

'Is it about the school, or is it about you?' Benji asked. He sometimes feared that, despite Siyue's commitment to child-centred education, a tiger mother lurked within her. He knew from his experiences with his students' own tiger parents that the knee-jerk reaction was to immediately lay into the teachers: that was part of the reason why Chinese schools were often so defensive.

'It just reminds me of the way my mother was with me,' she said, 'always taking the school's side whenever they criticised me, the teacher just saying "your kid is bad", which is a horrible thing to say. And my mum would never listen to my side of the story.'

Benji understood that Sulan's reaction had opened up Siyue's old wounds. 'This is about you and your mum, not just Eva,' he told her.

———

The arrival of the Covid pandemic at the beginning of 2020 shut down schools and tutoring centres alike. Eva's kindergarten closed, and Siyue and Sulan were forced to care for her full-time while Siyue figured out how to run her education company from home.

That early period of semi-lockdown was thankfully brief for most Beijingers; some residential compounds strictly limited guests, but Siyue's never did, and a few of her neighbours never stopped hosting dinner parties.

Initially, the government prevented outside visitors from entering Beijing until they completed a mandatory quarantine – and later relaxed this to a Covid test. For those who had reliable white-collar salaries and didn't have to travel much, life returned to normal relatively quickly. But the majority of migrant workers lost their livelihoods.

Siyue was part of the former group, but it was still an uphill battle to move her private education business online. Much of what she did relied on reading parents' and children's reactions, and responding to their needs on an emotional level during the fraught preparations for international school entrance exams. Siyue prided herself on her ability to know what clients wanted before they did, a skill that was highly valued by rich parents too busy to spend much time communicating with their children's various assistants and tutors.

Thankfully, her clients all agreed to a term of online classes and coaching sessions. Siyue knew they had been with her long enough to be committed to her services, but she also knew that if she had asked them for two terms online, some clients would have left. Luckily, Beijing allowed its schools to reopen a few months later.

At the start of Eva's second year of kindergarten, Sulan had wanted to take Eva back to her home town. It would be easier for all three of them, she argued, especially now that Siyue was even busier with her company. But Siyue had insisted they remain in Beijing. It meant more work, but that was a small price to pay to keep the family together.

———

Siyue often considered herself fortunate to be a single parent. One of her friends, who was going through a divorce, emphasised this to her: 'Siyue, you are so lucky. When you have a husband and a child, you have twice the burden of parenting.'

Though she believed the men in her friendship circle did more than most, they still did less than 50 per cent of the childcare in their marriages. Women were expected to manage the overall project and keep track of the tasks that weren't done.

All in all, Siyue felt lucky to be part of a two-woman team.

When she first moved to Beijing, Sulan had urged Siyue to find a husband, but after a while, she stopped. Sulan became acquainted with many of Siyue's female friends and often cooked them elaborate dinners of beef stew with bamboo shoots, as well as braised pork belly, cut into thick chunks with the gum-sticky skin still on. She was often quiet, a natural listener, but willing to offer her insights if asked. She didn't make unwelcome comments about anyone's weight or use of make-up. In return, the women opened up to her about their lives: their experiences of being single, what they did for work, and how they supported themselves.

Sulan's best friend in the compound was Eva's playmate's grandmother, who looked after her daughter and son-in-law as well as her granddaughter. She would complain to Sulan how tired she was every day; it wasn't just the number of mouths to feed, but that the mouths were prone to arguing in the ever-shifting dynamics of a household with three adults and one child. She would reminisce about the days when her daughter was single: 'What a good life we had back then!' she would say. Now she was always busy, and when she wasn't busy, she was exhausted.

When Eva went to kindergarten, Sulan had time on her hands. She spent it maintaining the online shop that Siyue had set up as a place for Sulan to channel her entrepreneurial energy. Sulan bulk-ordered and resold groceries that she liked: dried shiitake mushrooms, organic lavender soap, bunches of kale, boxes of whole frozen durian in their spiked shells.

One night, four years after she moved to Beijing to help care for Eva, Sulan suddenly said to Siyue: 'Why bother getting married? If you're a girl making money, in the modern world . . .' She trailed off, perhaps contemplating an alternate path through her own life.

14

The most unradical one
Sam

When she graduated from her master's course in sociology, Sam had the vague idea of looking for work at an NGO like the ones she had encountered in Shenzhen, where she had gone from hospital to hospital speaking to injured workers. She felt like she was one small fragment of society, but that she could contribute a little to changing it. NGO jobs were hard to come by, though, given the lack of funding in the sector, so she started volunteering as an editor for an up-and-coming left-wing blog called the New Commune.

The goal of the New Commune was to 'unite intellectuals, workers and farmers'. Its strapline spoke of utopias and collectives, but its published content dealt with everyday concerns, such as why working overtime was so common, or how employees could combat sexual harassment in the workplace.

Sam stayed in Shenzhen, but the New Commune's main office was in an apartment complex in Beijing, in such a remote quarter that it didn't feel like part of the city. To get there, Sam had to take a long subway ride and an overground train to the city's northern outskirts, where the landscape transformed from the business district's metallic skyscrapers into low-rise apartments and dry fields of yellow grass.

It was a cosy apartment. Two of Sam's colleagues lived in a bedroom adjacent to the office – or to put it another way, her colleagues had moved in together and turned their living room into an office. Most of the staff and volunteers were women in their early twenties. In the evenings, they ate dinner together in the living room/office, where they had two cats that played together on the floor.

Sam and her colleagues were trying to learn from political movements around the world to see what lessons they might apply to the Chinese situation. The two women who rented the flat had recently attended a conference of trade unions in Europe; they were surprised to find that they were some of the conference's only young, female attendees.

They also learned that, in Europe, the term 'left' had very different connotations from what it has in China, where it has a confusingly broad range, and can be used to refer to people who support the status quo of the Communist Party's rule, as well as to radical Maoists like Sam. In China's mainstream discourse, 'right' refers to those in favour of democracy and free markets, and is associated with a more internationalised, younger generation. In this respect, China's generational connotations of left and right were the opposite of what they stood for in the West: the 'left' was the conservative past, and the 'right' was the brave future.

Sam was interested in the history of the American labour movement, particularly the use of 'salting': the practice of entering a workplace with the goal of organising it. She often joked that, at the New Commune, she was in 'the most unradical part of the most radical movement' – the most radical edge, in her estimation, being the students who worked in factories after graduation to 'salt' them. Over the course of her master's degree and her time at the New Commune, Sam heard several rumours of students who had turned down elite employment prospects to do this work.

A small network of underground Maoist activists dedicated to 'salting' had taken root in the Pearl River Delta in the late 2000s. Salting was a much more radical tactic than those adopted by most Chinese labour NGOs, which, by the late 2010s – under pressure from the government – had, in order to survive, become more focused on helping individual workers obtain medical compensation or unpaid wages than organising workers collectively. Any form of movement-building attracted too much political scrutiny.

Sam admired the students who went to work in factories for their courage, but it wasn't the right path for her: she didn't consider herself tough enough. She couldn't stand for ten hours a day on a factory line, repeating the same minuscule movements thousands of times. She also didn't have much confidence in her ability to organise workers: her mannerisms and polite, roundabout way of speaking all betrayed the middle-class habits she found difficult to shake. Her interests and skills lay in thinking and writing, which is why her media job suited her.

Yet even this option, which she considered relatively tame, had its risks.

———

Barely a year after Sam started working at the New Commune, the police began hounding the landlord to kick her colleagues out of their Beijing office. The police frequently used this tactic with activists they didn't like but didn't have enough reason to arrest. It was never clear if their ultimate goal was to drive the activists to other cities, where they would become other police forces' problems, or simply remind them that, at any moment, the government could make their lives difficult.

Sam's blog had been hosted on the messaging app WeChat, which, by the mid-2010s, had become an all-encompassing social media, website-browsing and payments platform that comprised the majority of Chinese people's experience of the internet.

With the rise of social media, many political blogs flourished on WeChat's Public Accounts platform, threatening to transgress the unspoken boundaries of censorship. Some issues were clearly untouchable: the leadership's family wealth, for instance, and issues related to territorial integrity, like the future of Taiwan. But throughout the 2010s, the areas of sensitivity multiplied to the extent that editors could no longer predict the government's reaction to any piece of media with much accuracy.

It was common even for established newspapers to have an article blocked now and then. It was more devastating when an entire account was suspended for a period, although independent media outlets could weather these suspensions if they were relatively brief and they could hold onto their audience of dedicated readers. Sometimes, though, the consequences were more serious: in the spring of 2016, the labour news blog New Generation was permanently shut down after reporting on a strike of thousands of miners in China's post-industrial north-east, all of whom were owed wages by their state-owned enterprise.

Unlike New Generation, Sam's colleagues at the New Commune didn't cover breaking news; they mostly posted commentary and analysis from a Marxism-tinged perspective aimed at a young readership. But in the summer of 2016, they, too, were shut down by the online censors.

After a few months, Sam and her colleagues launched a new blog and attempted to recover their old readership. They printed tote bags bearing their new name, Today's Collective, and mailed them to their former subscribers. They had had to relocate their office, but their underlying pattern of writing and editing gave the team stability: whatever the circumstances, new posts had to be published and commissioned every week to maintain readers' interest. Eventually, the media outfit even secured enough funding to pay Sam a salary, although it was only a little more than what a delivery driver could make in Beijing. After living on a scholarship of Rmb12,000 per month during her master's degree, Sam was earning Rmb5,000–6,000 per month at the blog.

Sam opened their next office in Shenzhen. She shared the room with a young woman from another blog aimed at educating factory staff about workers' rights. Sam lived quietly in the office on the outskirts of her home city. She liked to take long walks along the harbour front facing Hong Kong. She saw a traditional Chinese medicine doctor to treat her easily inflamed skin, and carefully brewed her herbal prescriptions every day. When she wasn't editing, she was reading Buddhist scriptures, Marx or Lenin.

Later on, a more serious threat than the police approached one of Sam's colleagues – state security officers, who deal with matters of national importance. They didn't ask about Today's Collective, but the state security's presence in Sam's circles shocked them all. It showed them that they were on the edge of something the government considered dangerous.

———

In the summer of 2018, Sam started noticing articles on the various leftist social media accounts she followed about an unusual coalition of workers and students protesting in her home city.

In May 2018, Mi Jiuping, a worker at the Jasic Technology electronics factory in Shenzhen, had petitioned the factory to allow workers to unionise. Jasic's management, of course, refused to approve the application. In July, they retaliated by firing Jiuping and two fellow organisers. Undeterred, the workers tried to enter the factory again, at which point the management called the police. Jiuping and his fellow organisers spent a night in police detention. Their supporters protested outside the local police station – an unusually confrontational tactic. They, too, were detained for a night.

By this point, news of the labour dispute had filtered through the networks of Maoist activists into the broader communities of Marxist students across China's universities, some of whom started making their way south to Shenzhen.

A week later, on 27 July, Jiuping and his colleagues staged another protest outside Jasic. The police arrested thirty people, including one student activist, in what became the largest mass arrest of workers in three years. The next day, the Marxist students published an open letter calling on the local government to release the detainees.

Sam was impressed by their courage and the speed of their coordination and, feeling she had a duty to support them from afar, amplified their letter on her blog. Students flocked to Shenzhen and set up base in a rented dormitory in the city, calling themselves the Jasic Workers' Support Group.

Some of the students set about recruiting more students and supporters to come to Shenzhen. Others spoke to journalists, using media contacts shared by the broader, looser community of labour activists. Some devised plans for warding off their teachers and parents. At first, the police attempted to pressure the students by flying these guardians to Shenzhen and putting them up in hotels, where they would try to convince their children to abandon their campaign.

The students wore T-shirts printed with the black-and-white silhouettes of five arrested Jasic workers on the front. Below the image, in red lettering, the shirts declared 'Unity is Power'; the back read 'Jasic Workers, Stand Up, be Your Own Master, Establish the Union'.

One of the movement's most prominent student activists, Shen Mengyu, raised money to cover the group's legal costs through a WeChat crowdsourced payment page. Since all WeChat and bank accounts require verification, her real name was attached to her work. On the evening of 11 August, as she walked out of a restaurant where she'd had dinner with her parents, men in plain clothes seized her and forced her into an unmarked car.

At daybreak on 24 August, riot police stormed the students' dormitory and arrested the remaining fifty or so students, marking China's biggest student crackdown since Tiananmen Square. As the police searched their belongings, the students linked arms and sang the socialist anthem, the Internationale.

Later that day, a state media journalist for Xinhua News published a story accusing the students of being part of an illegal campaign controlled by foreign forces.

———

The crackdown on the Marxist students extended into the start of the academic year, at which point university administrators joined police in urging the students to abandon their activism. Pressure soon turned, once more, into violence: in November, an unmarked car drove into the campus of Peking University. Men wearing plain clothes grabbed two recent graduates who had been involved in the Jasic support group, beat them and dragged them into the car. The arrests of students and activists spanned five cities in total, stretching from Beijing to Guangzhou, Shenzhen, Shanghai and Wuhan.

In a surreal twist, China's top universities began banning their student Marxist societies. At Peking University, where Mao Zedong had once worked as a librarian and met with Marxist students in the late 1910s, the university administration replaced the Marxist society leaders with loyal party members. Overnight, a group that had once organised cleaners on campus became a study group for the sanitised government ideology of Xi Jinping Thought.

On a frosty late-December morning, Peking University's ousted student Marxist society leaders protested outside the university's Department of Marxism, linking arms to form a human chain. Teachers and guards wrestled them to the ground. For the rest of that day, the students were detained inside the same sociology classrooms that had hosted the labour studies summer camp Sam had attended years earlier.

———

Sam was in two minds about the student activists' tactics. She worried they had been too high-profile, too risky, and had drawn too much attention to themselves rather than the workers. But as police harassment of the students escalated, she felt she needed to support them in whatever small ways she could.

At the end of 2018, she began setting aside her editorial work at Today's Collective to help the students connect with other socialist groups, including the sub-factions of the Utopia forum she had once laughed at in high school. She asked these groups to take photos of themselves with banners, to sign petitions, to stage small demonstrations in parks. She hoped they would write about the Jasic disappearances on their blogs to spread awareness and show solidarity.

The groups she approached were of her grandparents' generation and represented a vast array of political tendencies within the broader labour movement. One of the grandfathers she visited had a photo of Xi Jinping on his wall. It was difficult to create unity: some even believed there was an element of truth to the Xinhua report that the students had been influenced by hostile 'foreign forces'. The Jasic students had split the Chinese labour movement: some feared the students' overt organising strategies would ultimately be counterproductive to the broader labour movement by making it more politically sensitive.

As she became more involved with the students, Sam's criticism of their tactics gave way to admiration. She saw how difficult it was to do what they were doing: to keep churning out posts for domestic blogs that reached large audiences before they were wiped by the censors and to keep their Twitter accounts alive for a foreign readership. To mobilise people with determination yet no end in sight. Sam thought the students were like a perpetual motion machine, constantly organising.

She felt it was her duty to show up for the activists who had graduated from university and remained in Shenzhen. On the occasions they gathered to work together, writing articles and contacting potential supporters, Sam would keep them company.

The organisers stayed in hostels that charged 10 renminbi per night, with three beds to a room, since the owners of such places tended to be lazy in applying the police rules for real-name identification of guests, only registering one identity card per group and not bothering with the rest. Other times, they slept on the plastic benches in the corners of 24-hour KFCs where the attendants never checked who was ordering. They worked until 2 a.m. and rose at 8 a.m. most days, surviving on diets of plain restaurant noodles with a dash of oil.

Sam lasted about two weeks in this lifestyle before she couldn't carry on, and took a step back.

———

After the arrests, some of the student activists were held in police detention centres, then released. Others disappeared into China's system of 'black jails', a network of extralegal detention centres reserved for those deemed threats to state security, officially called 'residential surveillance at a designated location' (RSDL). Police often hold detainees for up to a month before notifying their family members and up to six months before informing them of their crime. In RSDL, solitary confinement is a typical punishment, as is leaving bright lights on constantly to deprive the victim of sleep.

Both in the detention centres and in the black jails, the officers tried to manipulate the students to make scripted confessions, intimidating them one moment, then offering friendly, patronising advice the next. The officers assumed that everyone could be bought for a certain price or with enough force, even if that meant resorting to torture.

In January, police showed the Marxist students who had been released a video of those still detained. The students thought that the faces of their imprisoned colleagues looked swollen and colourless, their expressions unnatural. One male student said to the camera:

In our student society, we talked about the sixty-year history of the People's Republic of China . . . We exaggerated the beauty of the first thirty years after the revolution and the problems of the past thirty years after Reform and Opening Up. We were given a wrong view of history.

A well-trained male news anchor's voice suddenly blared over the video: *They used to think that China was not a socialist society, didn't approve of the current political system, and wanted to achieve so-called socialism through a student and workers' movement. After a period of reflection, how have their views changed?*

A female student said: *Now that I have been educated by the police, I truly understand China's national situation, in particular that, since the 18th Party Congress [when Xi Jinping was named as president], the party and the government have used many concrete methods to fight inequality.*

Shen Mengyu, the prominent activist who had been bundled into an unmarked car, said: *Our actions constituted illegal crimes, which not only seriously disturbed the social order, but also caused some foreign forces to use this incident to attack the party and the government, severely tarnishing China's international image.*

The male student spoke again: *Reform and Opening Up . . . was the correct developmental path, combining Marxism with China's special characteristics.*

A third female student's testimony concluded the video: *I will not only stand with my motherland and its people, I will stand with the party.*

———

As the months wore on, the police detention effort expanded to entrap other labour organisers, social workers, factory workers and NGO staff in the Pearl River Delta with no direct relationship to the original Jasic protests. The government seemed to be bluntly retaliating against the broader community of labour advocates.

Sam heard of more and more friends in her leftist circles being detained. The disappearances that hit her hardest were those of Wei Zhili and Ke Chengbing, who had co-edited the prominent labour issues blog, iLabour. She had admired their work, and had met up with them many times. While she was writing for Today's Collective, she had asked them for help on stories about the migrant workers who had built Shenzhen's skyscrapers and, as a result, were now dying from the lung disease silicosis.

She started feeling a mixture of paralysis and urgency for action. She thought that all she could do was show solidarity, but that was not enough. She eventually gave up nearly all her work at Today's Collective to focus on helping the student activists. (The blog had become less active anyhow, as many of its contributors were similarly absorbed by the student activist movement.)

With her media experience, Sam was chosen by an organiser within the movement to become one of the intermediaries between the students and the media. They needed someone to absorb the risk of being in touch with 'foreign forces'.

The organiser who had recruited Sam commanded a great deal of trust among the students. That meant Sam in turn was trusted, although nobody knew her name, and she knew very few other people's. That was one of the many rules of privacy that this band of underground activists used to keep themselves safe. But such rules also increased the isolation of its members, as well as the power of those higher up its hierarchy who knew more about what was happening within its structure.

————

When she went for walks on her own, Sam would dwell on the thought that the things she did for the movement weren't front line enough.

In the spring of 2019, she pivoted to providing immediate support for the labour activists who were being detained. She contacted their family members to ask about the circumstances of their disappearances and, if she could locate the activists, organised donations of money and food. She also looked for lawyers who could contact state security and pursue information about the activists' cases. Because very few human rights lawyers remained active in China after a wave of mass arrests in 2015, Sam sometimes resorted to hiring 'street lawyers', the kind who waited outside detention centres to offer their services to desperate clients.

Sam's sense of urgency slipped towards despair and then apathy. When she talked to her friends in the movement, she rarely brought up her growing sense of depression. It wasn't that she didn't talk about problems with her friends at all – she still fought to hold on to some of her old self-deprecating humour. It was more that, in her mind, the major struggles – politics and its burdens – lay outside the realm of everyday griping and commiseration. When she did talk about the worsening political situation, it was with resignation.

Part Four

15

The City Youth Community
June

In the summer of 2021, the online tutoring company that June worked for closed down her division. On a Friday in July, a leaked memo appeared on social media describing a complete government ban on for-profit tutoring in core academic subjects for children in compulsory education.

Known as the 'double reduction policy', the stated aim was to reduce students' volume of homework and cut after-school tuition costs for families. Investors started selling their shares in private tutoring companies immediately. The following day, state media confirmed that the most severe version of the rumours was true.

China's $120 billion private tutoring industry collapsed in value within a few days. The edutech company that employed June on their operations team had started the year with a market valuation of $38 billion; after the last weekend in July, it was worth less than $1 billion. Within a week, the regulatory deluge left millions of employees jobless.

The pace of change astonished everyone, but the storm had been brewing for some months. In March 2021, during a major annual government meeting, President Xi Jinping had described the disorder in the private tutoring industry as a 'disease'. The government imposed caps on tutoring fees. In May, regulators fined tutoring firms millions of dollars in total.

Around 10 million people had worked in China's private tutoring industry before its collapse, most of whom were young graduates like June. China's biggest private tutoring company, New Oriental, laid off two-thirds of their 100,000 staff. June estimated that her own firm took a similar hit, laying off 40,000 of its 60,000 employees.

Some tutors carried on teaching classes in private with the curtains closed. A video went viral of police kicking down a classroom door in Beijing and dragging a teacher away in front of his wide-eyed students.

In November, the founder of New Oriental, whose inspirational speeches June had listened to in her high-school years, who had exhorted listeners like June to 'hew a stone of hope out of a mountain of despair' – declared that the era of private tutoring had ended.

————

Luckily, thanks to her record of good appraisals, June was transferred to another part of the company that served university students, whose ages fell outside the scope of the new government regulations.

Though she was grateful to have a job, June was dissatisfied with her new manager, whom she felt was too inexperienced: she scored her as a 6, whereas in her eyes her previous boss had been a 10. Plus, like most people who had survived the lay-offs, June didn't trust the future of the private education industry. She started looking for new offers. After midnight, she'd lie in bed swiping on the Boss Zhipin app. She sent out hundreds of applications. She used the same strategy she had used to get her first job: sheer volume.

By the end of October, June had received several offers. She accepted one in the operations team of Paonow, a delivery services app that had recently become one of the country's most valuable publicly listed companies.

The average time a Chinese tech employee stays in their job is just eighteen months, and it pays to move around for higher salaries. At her first firm, one year out of university, June was making Rmb15,000 a month as a base salary, which went up to Rmb40,000 with commission. Paonow offered her even more. She and her boyfriend, Gaolin, moved into a flat that they had all to themselves.

June's new home was in the south-east of Beijing, about half an hour's drive from the city centre, in an industrial strip where the high-rise apartments of the Central Business District suddenly gave way to rows of red warehouses, which had once been part of a logistics hub. A private developer had converted these buildings into affordable housing for recent transplants, twenty-somethings like June who came from all over the country to work in Beijing. These compact loft-style units were branded the 'City Youth Community'. Several similar developments were strewn across the capital.

June spent her second Beijing winter in this compound. In the distance, beyond the perimeter wall of the warehouses, plumes of white smoke curled up from a factory smokestack and dissipated into the bright blue sky. The metal door of June's building opened to an endless corridor with brown plastic doors on either side. June's was at the end, almost thirty doors down on the left. She and Gaolin together paid Rmb3,000 a month for a snug unit whose linoleum tiles had underfloor heating. The rent was cheap for Beijing, but it was more than her sister made in a month in the garment factory she had worked at at June's age.

Though June had come a long way, she still didn't feel successful. The ladder of her life thus far mirrored China's geographical hierarchy: she had moved from her home village to a township, to the county town, to a city, to the capital city of her province, to the capital city of her country. Up until now, she had always been able to envision the next step. At twenty-two, she felt like she was stalling.

For the time being, June liked her job at Paonow well enough, and she was learning a lot from all the new people she met. Her role involved visiting Paonow's major business clients, from restaurants to clothing retailers. Sometimes she'd be stationed in their offices for a few days at a time, which brought a welcome degree of variety into her life. And outside work, June enjoyed the abundant opportunities Beijing afforded her to spark new friendships. Any one of her new acquaintances could become another Teacher Song: someone who could pull back a curtain to reveal an as yet unknown part of the world.

What was success, anyway? To June, it was about finding meaning in work and feeling a sense of progress and accomplishment. A year and a half in Beijing was hardly enough time to have achieved all those things, she reasoned.

June was quite content with her daily life in the City Youth Community, spending her Saturdays cooking in her compact flat while Gaolin worked. She would eat lunch sitting on her two-person couch in the space under the metal frame of her loft bed, with an electric hotpot on the coffee table in front of her bubbling with lamb broth. On Sundays, they both worked.

Gaolin was busiest at the weekends, since he gave private classes to children through the tutoring company he had joined. Despite initially feeling intimidated by the big city, Gaolin had got to like his Beijing life so much that June would sometimes rib him by suggesting they move back home.

On Saturday evenings, June would make a feast to eat with Gaolin, her favourite being hotpot. For this, she would prepare three different kinds of meat: thick slabs of mutton, chunks of lamb rib, thinly sliced curls of lamb, as well as plenty of greens, tofu, slabs of duck-blood jelly, and a steaming pot of rice. For a dip, she would mix together a bowl of chilli flakes and spices.

Often June would cook to music. Recently, she'd listened to a recording of Taylor Swift on her 'Reputation' tour in Dallas, Texas. On it, Taylor thanked her fans for spending their Saturday evening with her, amid all the things they could be doing instead in the big city.

Beijing, too, satisfied June with its abundant opportunities and possible friendships. It didn't give her a sense of belonging, but right now in her life, that didn't matter much. She prioritised learning, making money, doing something bigger. Maybe getting an MBA, and starting her own company.

June gave herself until she was thirty to fully absorb Beijing. After that, she thought she might move back to the capital city of her home province, where she and Gaolin had bought an apartment together after their first year of working in Beijing. In June of 2021, they had put a down payment of Rmb300,000 for a Rmb750,000 flat, thinking prices would continue to rise and that this would be the best way of investing their savings. The flat didn't yet exist; it was to be built by Evergrande, one of the country's biggest private property developers, over the next three years.

As was the norm in the industry, Evergrande had bought up land from local governments and borrowed money from state-owned banks in order to build new apartment blocks and sell them to customers. Many of these sales were uncompleted blocks.

Everyone from the local banks to the central government had a stake in the success of this growth model. But they vastly overestimated the demand for residences and shopping malls in smaller cities and towns, resulting in many of Evergrande's developments becoming ghost towers that would never be bought or completed. People referred to these structures as 'rotten-tail buildings', grey cement shells with gaping windows that stood on the edge of a city.

In September 2021, just three months after June and Gaolin sent their down payment to Evergrande, the company started missing its loan repayments. By then the property developer had become the most indebted in the world, owing more than $300 billion. Construction stalled, suppliers complained of missed payments, and customers complained of delayed apartment handovers.

Reading the headlines, June wondered if she and Gaolin would ever actually see their flat. Being an optimist, she thought that if their original apartment didn't work out, they'd make enough money to buy another one elsewhere. In the meantime, it didn't matter that construction had stalled, because they were happy living in Beijing, and they could afford their Rmb5,000 per month mortgage repayment.

Still, June knew it would be difficult for them to permanently settle in Beijing. House prices in the capital city of their home province were almost ten times cheaper than in their current neighbourhood, where they had little hope of ever owning a home. In addition to the prohibitive prices, migrants like June and Gaolin were forced to pay social insurance to Beijing's city government for at least five years in order to meet the minimum residence requirements to buy.

Although June was only twenty-two, she had also thought ahead to the problems of having children in Beijing. They would need a Beijing *hukou* to complete their schooling there. June would meet some of the requirements for a *hukou* if she got a PhD, but she didn't want to spend five more years of her life in a university. Nor did she want to sign a five-year contract with one of the state-owned enterprises that might give her a chance at the *hukou* lottery. Her twenties were fleeting and weightless, and June wanted to soar as high as she could before the heavy thud of motherhood came.

Some of June's older colleagues had settled in Tianjin, the port city two hours' drive away, where *hukous* were easier to obtain. Other young professionals went to Shenzhen or Guangzhou in the south. But June didn't want to settle for anything less than Beijing or Shanghai. If she was going to settle for a lesser city, she thought, she might as well move back to the capital of her province and be close to her family.

———

As 2022 arrived, June thought about her hopes for the year: finding greater satisfaction and success in her work.

Gaolin's hopes were better-defined. He hoped this would be the year they finally got engaged.

Gaolin's parents had been hurrying them to get married ever since graduation, following the Chinese maxim that dating in school was dangerously premature, relationships in university were a distraction from studying, but once you were out on the job market you needed to get hitched, as fast as possible. Marrying off their only son was how they discharged their responsibilities, handing their duty of care to his future wife.

June's father, on the other hand, wasn't looking forward to his youngest daughter getting married. In Chinese, a man 'receives' a wife, but a woman gets 'married out', like a parcel being shipped.

Gaolin often hinted at getting married. June had swerved the topic so many times that it left her feeling greasy, like she was leading him on. 'I don't think it's the right time' and 'Let's give it a few years' were her go-to lines, said softly, over and over again.

She could also be blunt: 'We're together, aren't we?' she once said.

'Yes,' Gaolin replied.

'Then what's there to worry about?'.

It wasn't that June didn't want to stay with Gaolin; she just didn't like the idea of marriage. It was another step towards forfeiting her independence. This year, Gaolin's parents were only pushing for marriage, but June knew that after the wedding they'd be pushing for children. She could stand her in-laws' questions about marriage, but she didn't want to be pressured into pregnancy.

June envisioned motherhood at some future stage – when she was in her forties, maybe – when she wouldn't be working so hard. She'd be financially secure and enjoying the fruits of her labour. She would live like Teacher Song, who volunteered at rural schools around the country, and travelled to a new destination at least once a year. She would let her kids do their own thing, and tell them not to bother her too much.

She didn't imagine the actual process of giving birth and raising small children. In fact, it scared her.

Maybe her fears came from her own childhood, she thought. Growing up wasn't easy, and she didn't want her kids to face the same difficulties she had. June had been initially separated from her mother by her mother's need to earn money in a faraway city, and they had been ultimately separated by a fatal workplace accident. She wished that her own children could grow up alongside her in Beijing, where they wouldn't get to class on their first day of middle school only to realise they were meant to know the English alphabet but didn't.

At the same time, June was grateful that the difficulties she had encountered had made her grow up faster and taught her how to take responsibility for her future. She sometimes judged the town-born kids of better-off relatives for their lack of ambition and motivation. *Did they have it too easy?*

She vowed never to hover over her kids like the helicopter parents whose children she had tutored to earn money at university. She didn't want to pay for private classes to try to buy their way to good grades. She didn't plan to 'inject them with chicken blood'. Her father had trouble even remembering which class she was in when he went to parent–teacher meetings at her school, and didn't know which university she had attended. That was fine by June. Looking after herself meant freedom, and she wanted her kids to have the same freedom – minus the pain it had cost her to get it.

16

Only money in my heart
Leiya

Leiya's centre for working mothers was at the end of the subway line, and stood in the quiet darkness of the migrant settlement beyond a neon-lit shopping centre. She had moved from their initial rented apartment to a larger, ground-floor shopfront in the same settlement. When Leiya had first arrived in this district of the city in the 2000s after leaving the factory dormitories to work at the workers' centre nearby, the settlement had been a patchwork of low-rises on the edge of the farmland, with open drains where wastewater flowed through the streets. Now it was a jumbled thicket of flats, leaning towards each other over narrow alleyways, as a result of being built by individual migant families one layer at a time; the locals called them 'handshake buildings'.

Directly opposite the centre was an electronics repair shop, where an old-style cathode-ray television was perched at the end of a wooden table, endlessly playing serialised dramas. The other shops in the alleyway were a microcosm of small-town China: a noodle joint with a stall out front displaying chopped-up ingredients, ready to stir-fry; traditional Chinese medicine shops; and a surprising density of hair and beauty salons, which some of the locals suspected were fronts for sex work.

Beyond this main alleyway lay many tiny paths that branched off at all angles, eventually leading up a hill, where they joined a larger road along the remaining electronics factories that hadn't been closed down in the great mid-2010s relocations. Sometimes this stretch of road held the smell of something deeply organic burning, like fertiliser. Sometimes, the smell was metallic.

At the peak of the hilltop stood a once-elegant compound with three-storey villas that had fallen into disrepair. It was a scene that was common in industrial outskirts like these. Countries like the UK had industrialised, then de-industrialised, over the course of two and a half centuries; southern China was doing so in the span of only four decades.

———

One summer night, Leiya assembled a dozen migrant women from the urban settlement for a workshop on how to gain school entry for their children. They sat on child-sized plastic stools in a shopfront open to the street, the indoor ceiling fans whirring in the humid air.

Leiya stood by the entrance under a banner that read: 'The Banyan Tree Centre: mutual support, equality and friendship.' Her yellow-and-white dog, Hanhan, trotted around, sniffing at newcomers. Whenever a man passed by the entrance he would bark loudly. Leiya wanted more men to come to the centre, but they rarely did, and Hanhan seemed to know this.

Leiya led a round of introductions that were simultaneously awkward and warm. The women, mostly in their early thirties, had been born in the countryside, and had come to the city to work as teenagers. They began their introductions with hesitation: 'I don't really know what to say . . .'

Then the words gathered speed, each mother confessing a variation on a familiar story to the assembled strangers: their struggle to keep their children by their side.

When the introductions came round to Leiya, she didn't hesitate. She described how eight years ago, out of personal necessity, she had started the community centre for working parents. Without a trace of the polite ambiguity that shrouds Chinese academics' discussions of such topics, Leiya named precisely the challenges migrant women faced.

'We're subject to the unfairness of this *hukou*-based society. Our kids need higher scores to go to school. And since the pandemic, I've been worried about our neighbourhood. It feels like everyone has been extremely anxious about finding work, paying for their children's education, affording rent, food . . . it all feels like it's only getting harder. So tonight, I'd like you to name your difficulties, and maybe we can find ways to help each other.'

'I wish my mother had had something like this when she was younger,' one woman said. 'I was also a left-behind child, and—' Before she could finish, the woman sitting in front of her burst into tears, her stooped shoulders trembling under her black nylon-lace dress.

'Come on, you haven't even sent your son home yet,' Leiya said, smiling at her. The tearful woman got up to get a tissue, and then sat back down, all the while softly apologising for her tears.

After the introductions, Nanfang dimmed the lights and presented a slideshow on how to pass the entry-level social worker qualification.

Nobody there was actually planning to become a social worker: they all had their own jobs in the nearby factories, the wholesale grocery market, childcare centres or as cleaners. As migrant mothers without local *hukou*, they were only interested in the school-entry points that came with such qualifications. To give their kids a chance at their school entrance exams, the mothers first had to pass a few tests of their own. Nanfang flicked through some slides of past questions.

Little Billy, age thirteen, has become withdrawn and stopped speaking at school with his teachers or classmates. His grandparents take care of him, and his parents call him on the phone now and again. His teacher has asked you to assess the situation. What kind of assessment do you give Billy?

Ms Zhang's daughter has passed away, and her relationship with her husband is deteriorating. He has been beating her. What is the best question to ask her?

'It's common sense, really,' said Nanfang, reading out the multiple-choice options. 'Get yourselves into groups to help each other go through the questions – we can cram together.'

Leiya's mother watched on, seated at a distance from those at the workshop. She had initially opposed her daughter's decision to give up her stable factory income to work in the more unpredictable world of labour NGOs. But as she observed the women chatting, she thought of how, when she was younger, she lacked the kind of support network that Leiya and her neighbours had created. She would sometimes say to Leiya: you don't know how good you women have it now.

The workshop finished around 10 p.m., and though many of the women had been up since 5 a.m., everyone stayed at the centre, gathering their chairs into small circles to chat. Leiya went out to pick up snacks for them. She returned with skewers of deep-fried bread balls, sliced squid and shiitake mushrooms, as well as purple mangosteens and a giant watermelon. Tonight's feast marked Qixi, the seventh day of the seventh lunar month: China's annual festival of romance.

'We got married on Qixi,' said the woman sitting at the head of some plastic children's tables pushed together to become a makeshift dining table. 'But we've never done anything to mark it. Not one flower, not one meal. Today's our tenth anniversary. If he doesn't at least send a red envelope of money, I'm not going home!' The table erupted in laughter.

'How do you get men to cook?' said another woman, who ran a beauty parlour nearby. 'You have to encourage them like little children. You say, my dear, this tastes great, you've done such a good job, it's just missing one flavour . . .'

For a few months, Leiya had tried launching a new venture to fund the centre: selling takeaway lunches. All the women who came to the centre already cooked every day, so Leiya reasoned they might as well capitalise on their skills. The migrant workers came from all over China's culinary map and were well versed in a wide range of cuisines, from the dry-spicy dishes of Hunan and the peppery punch of Sichuan to the sweet, gelatinous snacks of Guangdong and the south-east.

The women cooked together in the kitchen at the community centre, which had two gas-fire hobs. It was cramped and they had to move quickly to make things work. Selling the food, as with selling almost anything, was done online.

But for what price? The going rate for a simple workday lunch – typically a box of rice topped with something stir-fried in a sauce – was barely enough to generate the hourly wage to make it worthwhile. Restaurants could churn out the same dishes with lower overhead costs.

So Leiya designed their offerings to suit a higher price point: using cleaner ingredients, the women would make food that would theoretically appeal to a wealthier, more health-conscious demographic. But those customers proved difficult to find in Lion's Head Village – most families, like Leiya's, were focused on making ends meet.

Leiya's community centre had been funded by donations and payments from these mothers, as well as grants from local charity foundations. But the funding was drying up.

The drought had begun just before the enactment of China's Foreign NGO Law in 2017, which restricted the operations of foreign charities in China and their ability to fund local projects. Since the domestic philanthropic sector was still very immature, the Foreign NGO Law wiped out most of the funding available.

The pandemic brought the centre further problems. The harsh lockdown in Wuhan, where the virus started, initially contained the spread enough for other cities like Beijing and Shenzhen to get back to business quickly. But villages and smaller towns across China were more cautious and slower to reopen their borders, trapping the millions of migrant workers who had gone home for Chinese New Year away from their jobs. As a result, cities suffered labour shortages, and workers were forced to drain their savings. When the migrants of Lion's Head Village finally returned to the settlement, their bank accounts were severely depleted, with little money left over for donations.

They came back to a city whose employment opportunities had also shrunk. Many of the mothers of Lion's Head Village had been laid off from their factory jobs in the late 2010s, and now worked in the informal service sector as cleaners and caregivers. But the urban families who had employed them were also feeling the pinch. By the middle of 2020, one-tenth of urban residents had lost their jobs. And it was much easier to lose a casual job than a factory one.

Leiya used to pay herself and her one colleague, Nanfang, a monthly salary of Rmb4,000 each. By the first year of the pandemic, she could afford to keep paying Nanfang, but had to forgo her own salary. As a result, she became focused on new ways to earn money.

———

From the time she had founded the centre, Leiya had always worked various other part-time jobs to make ends meet. She had been a rental agent and an insurance salesperson before coming up with her own side gigs; although they were insecure, she preferred to have independence than a factory boss, as she'd had in her late teens. On the pull-down metal grille covering the side of the centre that opened onto the street, Leiya posted advertisements for her services. She used her childhood nickname, which made her sound like a multi-functional girl-next-door, someone who could meet any need:

LEILEI HOME SERVICES PLATFORM
Professional, committed staff to your door. Commercial
venue cleaning, home cleaning, cooking, childcare. Everyone
on our platform is vetted and trained.

LEILEI CONSULTING
Workplace disputes, *hukou* registration, school entry.
Contact professionally trained mediator Leilei.

A year after the pandemic began, during the Chinese New Year of February 2022, Leiya resolved to find full-time work. The funding for her community centre continued to dwindle, no new sources of grants were in sight, and her various inventive side gigs were failing along with the depressed local economy.

She would have to work during the day and attempt to run the centre in the evening and at weekends.

She began her search the usual way: by joining recruiters' groups on WeChat, where agents posted factory job adverts to hundreds of would-be workers:

NEW! Sharp Electronics | Seeking both men and women | Age 18–40 | No underage worker inspections | 12-hour shifts, rotating night and day shift | Monthly wages Rmb4000–6000 | Includes dormitory and factory campus bus | Lots of ways of earning extra | Ask for more details | Offline interviews | Staying in the dormitories requires a Covid test every 24 hours | Also mass recruiting casual workers, student interns.

NEW! Jicond Food | Men and women age 18–38 | Option 1: Work for 10 days, become short-term staff, Rmb240/day, contract period of 3 months. No wages if you work for less than 7 days. Wages paid on the 15th of every month. | Option 2: Rotating day and night shifts, men and women, after working 45 days get Rmb7,000 back plus Rmb600, work hours 7 a.m.–7 p.m., most workers get more than Rmb6,000 per month.

The adverts sometimes offered bonuses to workers who stuck it out for more than a week. Migrant workers often calculated their income by the day, and would move between factories every month or more frequently.

They left because the jobs weren't good enough to make staying worthwhile. Some of this floating population of workers looked for short-term contracts because they were suspicious of abusive factory bosses and didn't want to commit to longer contracts where wages might be withheld. Others grew impatient with the tedium of repetitive labour. With limited routes for promotion, and few opportunities for training, switching factories was one of the only means of exerting control.

By the early 2020s, the cost of living in cities, even in urban settlements, had become so steep that the low-skilled factory jobs that had boomed in the 2000s no longer made economic sense. Desperate for cheap labour, some factories offered one-day contracts, giving the worker the freedom to walk away at any point, so long as they didn't mind living without social insurance. Others hired temporary workers from dispatch agencies, who moved on every few weeks, thus avoiding making social insurance payments.

Once the country's bedrock for employing low-skilled workers, the manufacturing sector became casualised. Its biggest competition for hiring became the informal service sector, or so-called gig economy: platform jobs for delivery riders and ride-sharing drivers like Leiya's friend Yulan, whose daughter was in the same school year as Xinling.

Leiya had also downloaded the driver's version of the Didi ride-hailing app. But before trying it out, she wanted to hear about Yulan's experience first.

They arranged to meet at the spicy Sichuanese canteen near the community centre for lunch. Leiya had been helping Yulan with high-school entry. Yulan didn't have a local *hukou*, meaning her daughter would have to get much better marks than Leiya's in order to get into the same state-run high schools.

Soon after Leiya had sat down at the restaurant, Yulan walked in.

'I can't find it, I really can't,' said Yulan, sitting down, and placed two mottled-red pomegranates on the table. Leiya turned one over: there was a patch of black mould.

'*Aiya!* And these were expensive ones too,' Yulan said. Leiya stuck the tip of her chopstick into one, and dark juice seeped out of the wound. She tore open the thick skin, fragment by fragment, working her tool slowly.

'It must be at our old home,' Yulan continued. 'I gave the birth certificate to my great-grandfather for safekeeping, but he passed away, and then our great-uncle did . . . there's nobody left in our old home. The grass is a metre tall.'

Yulan handed over a plastic folder thick with printed forms and tiny booklets in cloth-bound covers. It contained the official histories of her and her husband, from the village to the city: births, residence permits, social insurance payments. Just not the one certificate her daughter needed to go to school.

For the past ten days, Yulan had been getting up at 5 a.m. to charge her rented electric car, and then clock into the Didi ride-sharing app. It was one of the many online platforms that had become ubiquitous in the mid-2010s by pooling contract-free migrant labour and providing it to customers instantaneously.

Business at the home renovation company that Yulan and her husband ran was deteriorating, and so were their arguments. In the early months of the pandemic in 2020, Yulan decided to make money on her own. Her target, which she rarely met, was to make Rmb500 a day. She slept in the car when there were no passengers, and finished at midnight.

But as she and Leiya ordered lunch in the middle of Yulan's nineteen-hour work day, Yulan was her usual riot of storytelling. On her first day on the job, she had run into a male taxi driver who told her he was an 'old hand', and offered to help her with any problems she faced.

A few mornings after that, he'd asked if she would have breakfast with him. She'd said no.

A few days later, he'd sent her a digital red envelope of money on WeChat. 'What's this?' she'd asked him. 'You won't eat breakfast with me, so I wanted to give you some breakfast money,' he'd said.

'He likes you,' Leiya said.

'So what?' said Yulan. 'In my heart there's only money!'

Yulan went back with Leiya to the community centre, where she took a nap while Leiya and Nanfang talked.

Half an hour later, Yulan wandered over and started chirpily joining in the conversation while nibbling at the grapes on the table.

'Not rushing out to drive any more?' Leiya asked, teasing her. 'When you're happy, you forget all about money!'

Yulan had wanted two children, but her husband and mother-in-law had wanted three, and that's how many she took care of. She wanted to apply for a city *hukou* so her kids could have guaranteed places at state schools. Her husband didn't want to change his own *hukou*, so she had to do it.

'Someone with views like his will never change,' she said, sighing. 'He says his ancestors are from there, so that's where his *hukou* stays. He doesn't take care of the kids at all. The only thing he does for us is earn money. Never mind, when I'm rich I'll get rid of him!'

———

One evening, Yulan had been taking a Didi passenger to a remote part of the city she'd never been to before, and was worried she wouldn't be able to pick up another passenger when she got there. She remembered the driver who had bought her breakfast and volunteered his help whenever she needed it. Tapping open their WeChat conversation history, she saw the string of unreplied-to voice messages he'd sent her over several weeks, most of which she'd not bothered listening to.

Didi drivers liked to message each other using voice recordings only, so that they could talk and drive at the same time. The most talkative liked to drive while receiving a constant stream of voice messages from WeChat groups of several hundred drivers, exchanging tips about where to find the most passengers and where the traffic police tend to pull over drivers without local *hukou*.

Yulan recorded her very first message to him: 'Hey, I'm heading to this place. Is it hard to pick up orders there?'

A little red exclamation mark popped up next to her unsent message, showing that he had deleted her contact. Although she had been the one who had spurned him, Yulan was furious.

The next morning, at their local charging garage, Yulan confronted the driver.

'Why did you delete my contact?' she yelled at him, startling everyone at the garage in their 5 a.m. muddle.

'You never replied to me!' he said, partly taken aback by her attack, partly quite pleased that she had said something to him for the first time in weeks. 'But,' he quickly added, seeing his chance, 'I can add you again?'

'Even if you tried to add me, I wouldn't accept it,' Yulan shot back. She said nothing to him for the remaining hour her rented electric car took to charge.

———

Yulan started her days in the charging garage at 5 a.m., just in time to catch an hour of the cheaper electricity rates and be ready for the morning rush hour. Charging stations were where Yulan gathered the intelligence she needed for a successful day's driving: where there were the most passengers, where she could park without getting fined, where it was safe to take a nap, where there were public bathrooms.

In the year since Yulan had started driving for the Didi ride-sharing platform, she had learned her own tricks: to put a bag on the front seat, so that passengers couldn't sit there and then try to put their hand on her thigh. To drink less water, and to go to the toilet whenever there was the chance. One time when she was bursting to go, she'd been with a passenger when she had driven past a public bathroom. She'd asked her passenger if she could quickly slip in, and she'd replied, 'No, just go in the bushes when you get to my destination.' Go in the bushes? Did she think she was a dog?

––––––

Yulan had signed up for Didi because her aunt Tingting had been driving on the platform, and had heartily recommended it. It would give her freedom, Tingting had told Yulan, she could set her own hours. Now Yulan sometimes wondered why Tingting had been so enthusiastic. She warned Leiya that being a ride-hailing driver meant freedom at too high a price.

Being a driver meant being chained to Didi's points system. Drivers were awarded points for good behaviour, such as clocking in during the morning, lunchtime and afternoon rush hours every day. Drivers in the same area competed with each other, and the platform prioritised sending passengers to the drivers with the highest points. You needed a minimum number of points for the platform to send you a good volume of orders.

Yulan did, however, love chatting to her passengers. Some would strike up a conversation with 'Wow, you're a female driver', and Yulan would reply, 'There are more and more of us these days.' Because of the pandemic downturn, women had ventured into traditionally male industries. Usually Yulan would be the first one to speak. After reading off the phone number on the order to check she had the right passenger, she would look at their destination and say something like, 'So you're going to the office?' She remembered her passengers with the funniest stories and the ones she had long conversations about parenting with. Talking made the journey fly by.

She didn't like it when her long-distance passengers didn't speak, and she didn't like the ones that opened their Douyin app as soon as they climbed in, their phone speakers giving out repeat bursts of the same pop song as they swiped through their short-video feed.

Chatting also got her private clients, which were essential for having a regular flow of income, especially now that the platform was sending her fewer orders.

Yulan knew why she was being punished by the algorithm. On Halloween, when revellers had flocked into one of the city's vast shopping complexes and the traffic was terrible, she'd cancelled an order to avoid getting a parking fine by being stuck in the complex. Didi sent her a message telling her she had had 12 points deducted, the worst penalty possible short of being suspended. Now she was at the bottom of the pile.

———

Hearing Yulan's advice, Leiya decided against driving for Didi. The clincher was that gig platforms didn't provide social insurance. For migrant workers with no plan of getting a local *hukou*, social insurance was almost useless. But Leiya had a local *hukou*, and had spent years extolling the importance of social insurance for receiving pensions and health care.

In her WeChat jobseekers' groups, she added labour dispatch agents and quizzed them about their insurance provisions. But recruiters were known to be liars. In the first job Leiya found, printing and adding up orders for a takeaway platform, the agent promised her that social insurance was included, along with monthly wages of Rmb5,000. She went for an interview at the company, and confirmed with the hiring manager that she'd get social insurance. She worked there for a few days before signing a contract. When she did, her manager told her she'd only get social insurance after three months' work, and asked her to sign an agreement saying she was voluntarily giving up the missing insurance payments.

Leiya fought back. She said she wouldn't sign the agreement and that she had a legal right to insurance. 'That's just the way it is with our company,' the manager kept repeating. 'This is normal; nobody gets insurance.' They had hired several workers at the same time as Leiya, he said, and they couldn't make an exception for her.

Next, the manager offered Leiya a probation period of a month, unwaged and without insurance, after which she would get both pay and insurance. Even then, the amount of insurance they offered to pay was based on a much lower wage than the one she was actually paid – a common trick in order to reduce the employer's contributions. Her monthly wage according to her contract was Rmb2,300, the regional minimum wage. Her manager promised her that with bonuses added on she'd get at least the Rmb5,000 that was advertised.

Again, she threw the offer back at them. She knew they were looking for illegal ways of cutting their costs at every turn. So she quit after four days, getting a few hundred renminbi for her trouble – way less than the wage she had been promised, but better than the nothing that workers often got for walking away early.

For her next job, Leiya looked on a job-listings website, and got an interview at an electronics factory. This time she wasn't on the assembly line; her computer skills qualified her to work in the operations office. She went six days a week, from 8 a.m. to 5.30 p.m., often staying later.

Leiya's base monthly salary was Rmb5,000, and her total pay was about double that, if she added on bonuses and commission, as well as deductions for taking days off. She was glad they provided lunch, and her manager was reasonable to negotiate with. Her commission was based on her output, but she wasn't sure how this was measured. The biggest problem was rest days. Leiya wanted the weekend off to work at the community centre, while her manager didn't want her to work less than six days a week, so instead she had to forego wages on the extra days she went to the centre.

For Leiya, keeping the community centre going was the priority. She had survived for fifteen years in precarious civil-society organisations; many of them had gone under, but the people and the ideas survived, by and large. Most of her life's downturns and upturns had been unpredictable, from the day she had bluffed her way into her first job as an underage worker, to the day she went to her first workshop on feminism.

But the local economy had never been as bad as it was now. She knew that her factory job wasn't permanent, and that she had only chosen it to tide her and the centre over during the economic downturn. She only hoped it was a downturn, rather than the future.

17

Sandcastle on the shore
Siyue

During the first few months of the government crackdown on private tutoring, Siyue found that her stress over the near collapse of her education company had manifested as physical tension in her body. One afternoon, her neck and shoulder seized up to the point that she was barely able to rotate her head. Siyue decided she needed to delve deeper into herself, to do things others might consider hippy-dippy or mystical. In times of challenge, she thought, she needed to expand her mind.

While her mother looked after Eva, Siyue went to see an acupuncturist, who pressed thin needles into her meridians. She lay on the acupuncture bench for half an hour, basking under the heat of the infrared lamp. She went to her traditional Chinese medicine doctor, and for Chinese massage. She went to see a hypnotist, to try to reach a space inaccessible to her conscious mind, and had a vision of other lives she might have lived.

In this vision, Siyue was an ambitious woman in imperial China. She wanted to take over her father's business, but knew she had to marry to legitimise herself in a male-dominated society. So she married for convenience, and barely noticed her husband, who stood by her side helping out as she balanced her giant accounting books every day.

She was so successful that the emperor became jealous of her wealth, and looked for any reason to take it from her. Soldiers arrived at her home to execute her, and her husband ran out to defend her. In that moment, she suddenly realised that the man who had quietly stood by her side was willing to die for her, and truly loved her. She realised that she loved him too, and that there was no point in surviving if he was to sacrifice himself.

After the soldiers killed him, she ran into their swords and died instantly, painlessly. She felt her soul and the soul of her husband floating up to heaven hand in hand, and she thought: *If I'd realised it was so easy, I would've gone ahead and died earlier.* In that moment, she did not fear death. She felt bold and weightless.

As she entered Heaven, she saw the Mother Goddess of Chinese mythology, Wangmu Niangniang, dressed in floating robes that encircled her like clouds. Wangmu Niangniang spoke to her in English with a British accent.

'Back again?' she said. 'Silly girl. You're always so bored up here, I wanted to give you a life where you could have some fun.'

———

After the July crackdown on private education, Siyue lost two-thirds of her staff in one weekend; some left voluntarily, some were furloughed, some she had to dismiss. By the end of the year, her full-time team had shrunk to a fifth of its former size, from sixty to twelve. She spent the autumn term trying to protect her colleagues' jobs for as long as possible until they found other jobs.

In the meantime, Siyue attempted to maintain the parts of her enterprise that she deemed safe enough to run. Thankfully, well before the crackdown, she and her co-founder Benji had been trying out other ideas. They had developed a consultancy arm of their business that gave advice to local schools, which continued to serve a steady stream of clients. The consultancy grew healthily, carrying the rest of the business along with it.

Siyue was also running a programme that she called 'holistic academic support', which essentially amounted to family counselling. In general, Chinese parents born in the 1970s were still too unfamiliar with the concept of mental health to seek therapy unless their children were on the verge of suicide, but counselling under the guise of university entrance preparation was more appealing. Most of the time, Siyue's role was to gently advocate for the child amid a barrage of criticism from their parents, but she showed the parents she understood their concerns as well. She allowed her instincts to guide her through their conflicts, sensing what each party might need in a given moment.

This support programme still teetered on the edge of what was considered legal in the eyes of the authorities. If a foreigner like Benji was present in a support session with a child, then it could be considered an English lesson, and thus illegal. If too many children were present, it was considered a group class, also illegal. The regulators could drop in at any time: one day, Siyue's learning centre was visited by eighteen different police and local government officers.

The learning centre had been an experiment in a new, more holistic style of education, one possible only for a short window in the country's history when there was both regulatory openness and a steady supply of parents with the money and willingness to try new things. Now Siyue had to close its doors, much to the dismay of the students for whom it had been a safe space. Some weeks after the centre's last day, the teachers found a student wandering aimlessly around the entrance.

Siyue's impressive network of female allies was, as ever, her main support system during this time. One of her friends, whom she felt was like a big sister to her, often asked Siyue if she needed any help with money. She asked it casually, without implying there was any shame or pity involved. Siyue had always made herself open to giving and receiving help from her friends and was grateful for her friend's willingness to help. Another friend, a fellow entrepreneur in the education industry, referred her own clients to Siyue. Others helped her hunt for new colleagues, as well as bringing her other important contacts. When Siyue needed a pick-me-up, she'd call another friend, a professional counsellor, who would give her impromptu coaching over the phone.

Her search for a new office space was aided by yet another female friend who ran her own consultancy out of a villa, and offered Siyue one floor of the building for a low rent. It was much smaller than the old learning centre, but Siyue's company was downsizing. Inside, the villa was furnished like a stately English home: mahogany tables and heavy leather chairs, staircases with dark wooden bannisters. Siyue's friend was starting a new project helping the second and third generations of rich Chinese families maintain their wealth, and together they planned a collaboration that would teach these parents how to not only save for their children's futures but also invest them with intrinsic motivation, resilience and sound values.

One lunchtime in the middle of the Beijing winter, Siyue sat on the villa's terrace, the sunlight warming her in its crisp glare. She reflected on how the crisis had made her want to stew over perceived betrayals, but she knew she needed to resist this tendency.

She was thinking of a colleague who had left the company shortly after the crackdown. Siyue had felt hurt; she'd thought the colleague would stick by them, and become a future leader. Another colleague had reminded her: 'Siyue, you don't own anyone!' and in that moment she'd thought, 'Yes, that's true.'

She owned nobody, and she was increasingly wondering if she owned anything. Though she was grateful for a new venture in which to channel her knowledge and energy, Siyue was deeply shaken by the crackdown. She and Benji had invested so much time and energy into the company over the past seven years, and it had all been demolished over one weekend by one regulatory notice. She and her teachers had developed so many lesson plans to be used by new students for years into the future. At her most pessimistic, she wondered whether it would ever be worth investing in any future venture if it could all be so easily washed away like a sandcastle on the shore.

But in other moments, when she stepped back from the carnage of it all, Siyue was strangely glad about the crackdown on private tutoring, because she had been feeling increasingly out of alignment with the industry. The year before the pandemic, Siyue's company had reached an all-time high with clients. She had started to feel that her wished-for clientele of parents aligned with her holistic-education values was getting diluted with those who were just there for the English tuition, and that she was doing all the important work, the work of mentoring and counselling students, in her spare time. The emotional skills that she paid attention to were too subtle for many families to understand if they only cared about the short-term return on investment: higher exam scores.

The industry was rife with exploitative sales practices that preyed upon parents' insecurities and vulnerabilities. Her fellow entrepreneurs regarded the reforms with a mixture of despair and begrudging acknowledgement that there was, as President Xi put it, a 'chronic disease' at the heart of the tutoring industry. Nobody liked the strong-arm sales tactics, and nobody wanted their own children to be squeezed through the same machine.

Yet the reforms didn't solve the essential problem: families still experienced the education system as a prisoner's dilemma of competitive cramming. Those who could afford it carried on hiring tutors in private, hoping to gain an advantage over those who didn't. One consequence of the reforms was to extend the power of the Education Ministry, police and local government by giving them another opportunity to extract fines.

———

The first two years of the Covid pandemic had been relatively gentle for Beijingers, thanks to the zero-Covid policy that contained outbreaks in other towns, leaving Beijing free from city-wide lockdowns. Residents lived under the Covid-tracking apparatus: getting throat swabs and test certificates before boarding a train, endlessly scanning QR codes in the entrances of buildings to log their visits, and showing security guards their 'Health Kit' apps, which displayed a traffic-light colour indicating whether the individual had recently visited any risky areas. Siyue's daughter Eva and her friends invented a new game of tag called 'Security Guard' in which one kid would catch the others and demand to see their Health Kit app. At four years old, they had grown up under the pandemic controls: for them, this was normal.

But in April 2022, the highly contagious Omicron variant started spreading in the city, and Beijing's workplaces and schools were forced into a partial lockdown.

After a disorientating start to working from home, Siyue began to enjoy spending more time with her neighbours, a community of upper-middle-class professionals from around the world who were generous with one another. The neighbour who lived opposite gave Eva the little dresses her own daughter had grown out of. Another neighbour, a few floors down, often brought Siyue organic fruit and vegetables.

It was in the middle of the lockdown, while Siyue was working from home, that she and her neighbours received the news that their entire apartment block was being sold, and they would be forced to leave within a few months. Siyue went for a walk to try to digest the news in the compound garden, which by then was balmy with the early-summer sun, before telling her mother and Eva. She needed to absorb the shock of such a change first; otherwise, her mother's anxiety would only amplify her own.

Siyue and Benji gathered with their other friends in the compound to discuss their options. Some began looking for apartments in other towers within the same compound; others took this as the final sign that they should leave the capital city for a softer life in their home towns. Others, with foreign connections, were planning to leave China altogether.

The parents in the compound talked about how their children had become more needy recently, acting out during the day and clinging to them at bedtimes. One of Siyue's teacher friends suggested the reason: 'They go to school, then they don't. They take a Covid test every day, then they don't. They have no routine. The only certainty in their life is you, the parents. They're needy because everything is changing.'

For Benji, the building's sale threw Beijing's class divisions into sharp relief. He thought of one of his and Siyue's former employees, a woman in her early thirties who had left the company after the crackdown the previous summer and stopped working entirely. She had had the option to quit because her family owned half a dozen apartments in Beijing. It wasn't that her parents were exceptionally wealthy; they were just old Beijingers who had bought property twenty years ago, at the start of the real-estate boom. There was a level of wealth that meant you could 'lay flat' – the Chinese slang term for opting out of the rat race – and still do well.

For everyone else, whose income came from their wages rather than inherited assets, Benji felt life was too often a never-ending challenge to stay ahead of the curve. His own experiences were at odds with the values he sought to instil in his students and their parents about prioritising their interests and well-being over the urge to cram to get ahead. How can you change yourself and your children within such a system if the system stays the same?

Siyue reminded Benji that children adapt quickly. They are versatile; they find new routines. As adults, we often forget that, she told him. Our role is to show them how to create new things, to take charge of their own life stories. Siyue expected life would give her hardships, but that it would also bring her the friendships and community she needed to survive them. For her, it all came down to Magda Gerber's most basic teaching: humans are hardwired for connection. It had been eighteen years since Siyue first left home, betraying her father's plan for her by studying English in an unknown city that had showered her with serendipity.

Siyue saw the disproportionate adversity she had faced in life as a blessing. If she hadn't been shamed by her mother and teachers at primary school, if she hadn't dropped out of college, she might never have developed her passion for transforming education. She often thought of the quote by the ancient Chinese philosopher Mencius:

When Heaven is about to confer a great mission on any woman, it first exercises her mind with suffering, and her sinews and bones with toil. It exposes her body to hunger, subjects her to poverty, and hinders her undertakings. By all these methods it awakens her heart, hardens her resolve, and grows her abilities.

In other words, those with a predestined mission are meant to endure suffering so that they might emerge better equipped to fulfil their life's purpose. Though Siyue's life had been upended by the pandemic and the crackdown, she still believed she had a fundamental purpose: to save children from their parents.

18

The belly she came from
Leiya

As the autumn term began, Leiya was trying to recruit volunteers for the Opening Page project, an initiative run by a charity that worked with migrant families. Opening Page encouraged parents to read to their children. Leiya knew that verbal skills in early childhood were one of the most important determinants of educational success. Reading to toddlers, even before they could speak themselves, shaped their language acquisition and brain development for the rest of their lives. Yet the mothers in Leiya's community had the least time and capacity to do so.

It was difficult for Leiya to find mothers to take part in Opening Page, squeezing it between their cleaning jobs or their factory shifts. In a previous workshop her centre had held on the importance of early-childhood development, she'd found that the attendees were mostly wealthier mothers from a nearby neighbourhood. She wanted to find working-class mothers from her urban settlement for Opening Page. Through constantly asking around, she eventually found enough mothers to meet the minimum class size of sixteen to take part in the project.

On Sunday afternoons, the mothers met with teachers who guided them in the art of story-reading. The mothers, born after the 1980s, were all literate, but most found it awkward to read aloud, and even more difficult to be playful when acting out different characters. They read hesitantly, whereas the Opening Page teachers injected drama into their readings. The children could tell the difference: at the sound of a confident narrator, even the infants in the group stopped to look up at the trainer. When the trainer asked a question, they all clamoured to be the first one to answer.

Eventually, the teachers hoped the mothers would lead their own reading groups, creating a ripple effect. At the end of the project, the charitable foundation gifted them bags of books, and Leiya organised a graduation ceremony: a karaoke party.

———

After lunch on Sunday, Leiya walked out of the centre and wove her way through the alleyways of the migrant village, collecting mothers as she went until they were a gang of twenty or so. She stopped at a bakery, where she bought two boxes of green-bean cakes, freshly pressed and ringed with toasted sesame seeds. At the corner shop, the group bought litre bottles of fizzy soda and sweet iced tea, and buried them deep in their backpacks in order to smuggle them into the karaoke parlour.

Inside the parlour, choosing songs was painfully cumbersome, as it is at the beginning of every karaoke party, each singer unsure of the right moment to unleash their taste on their friends. One of the younger women, wearing a dark dress, wanted electro-pop dance anthems; Leiya, in her usual sweatpants and T-shirt, looked for classic folk ballads.

Let's go charge to the dock!
I'll be leaving you very soon.
The sound of the steam whistle drowns out my sorrow,
and the tears that I cannot stop.

It's not that I don't love you;
it's because I'm from the village.
One year's income is barely enough to keep me alive,
never mind take care of you.

I will go and strive for you,
no matter how tough, how tired, I won't look back.
So long as you patiently wait for me,
there'll always be the day I turn up.

Wait until I've moved into the city,
and drive a Mercedes-Benz to pick you up.
Then I'll draw you into my arms,
and once more call you my darling.

After three hours of singing, Leiya cut the music and performed the graduation ceremony. She read out the list of names, and one by one the women went up to take a photo with her, holding a certificate. She handed them each a gift bag. As they left the karaoke booth, the women looked inside the bags to find they contained a pack of sheer tights and – to everyone's amusement – a box of condoms. It was a few months after the government had announced it would be relaxing the cap on children to three, as part of a bid to encourage women to have more children.

'Are we still allowed to give these out?' someone asked, giggling.

'The local village committee was giving them out a while ago,' said Leiya, as if she were defending herself to a government official; working in community organisations for almost two decades had made her well versed in dealing with accusations of having improper politics.

'Yeah, but they must have been really old by then. You'd better double-check every one. Make sure there aren't any pinpricks,' someone else joked.

The three-child policy announcement had been met with an unusually harsh wave of online criticism from tired mothers. Rather than being seen as permission to have more children, everyone saw it as a sign of looming government pressure on women to rescue the country's plummeting birth rate.

Leiya led everyone from the karaoke parlour to the local Sichuanese restaurant. She ordered the kind of dishes that stretch a long way because they pair deliciously with large amounts of rice: heavily flavoured pickles, salted vegetables, spicy fish, which altogether cost barely more than Rmb20 a head.

As the dishes arrived, one of the women gave her assessment of the country's birth rate: 'Kids nowadays don't get married because they're too smart. They weigh up the pros and cons. We were all stupid when we got married.' She paused to reflect. 'Young people need to be stupid, too. It's best to be dumb at love and clever at work.'

———

After dinner Leiya walked home on her own, through the deep underpass that still held splodges of grey water despite it not having rained for a month. Her mind turned to her daughter Xinling, who was turning fourteen soon, and was in her second year of middle school: the next year would be her final one.

The more she thought about it, the more the light of the day's celebrations faded. Of all the challenges she had faced in her life so far, she felt most hopeless about Xinling's *zhongkao*, the high-school entrance exams that mark the end of nine years of compulsory education, and separate students into two educational pathways: academic and vocational. Half of all sixteen-year-olds get into academic high schools, and the rest enter vocational schools or leave school altogether for work. But Leiya, like many parents across China, didn't see vocational school as an option for her daughter. She saw it as a failure.

The kids who ended up in vocational colleges also knew that was how they were seen by society. They were used to having their teachers give up on them; in turn, they gave up on themselves. The vocational colleges' instructors often had the same attitude. At a vocational school near Leiya's home, one teacher described the place as a 'trash recycling station'. It is a social sorting station as well: more than 70 per cent of vocational students are from rural families, and their parents are often manual labourers.

China had rapidly licensed thousands of new vocational schools over the past two decades, enough to hold 10 million students a year. The government wanted to model them on the German vocational training system, in which companies and schools partner to train secondary-school graduates. But the hastily built system at best provided a holding pen for China's rural and small-town children, and at worst forced them to work at factories when the local government needed a ready supply of cheap labour.

Leiya remembered the vocational students she had met while working at the City Workers' Community Centre in the 2000s, before her daughter was born. The centre's staff visited hospitals to offer support to victims of workplace injuries, and every so often Leiya would come across a teenager not yet old enough to work, whose vocational school had forced them onto the assembly line.

She had met a dozen of these hospitalised teenagers over the years, including some from her home province. She knew how unsettled and out of their depth they must have felt: she, too, had started working at fifteen, when she had followed her parents to Shenzhen and decided not to return to her village school. She had bluffed her way into her first factory job, underage.

But *she* had made the choice. She had chosen the city and its stuffy factories – and it had been her choice, too, whenever she had resigned and left behind sleazy managers or exhausting work schedules. In a forced internship, the vocational school's teachers often followed their students to the factories to discipline them. They threatened the students that if they left, they would not be able to graduate, meaning their three years' worth of tuition fees would have been for nothing.

Leiya thought that the factories sometimes got in touch with the schools to recruit students, and she suspected the teachers got a cut. The students were a flock of casual labourers, easily herded from place to place and ultimately disposable. In the electronics supply chain, major buyers like Apple and Amazon wanted new goods produced each season, and factories needed a supply of flexible workers to bring in during peak periods like the pre-Christmas rush.

When a student got injured on the assembly line, neither the factories nor the schools would take responsibility. Since factories don't have formal labour contracts with students, it's easy for them to avoid blame. In the end, as Leiya put it, things were 'settled by being left unsettled'. The factory and the school might privately pay a small sum to the student's family before quietly shuffling the other students back to their classes.

'Anyone can become cheap labour,' Leiya would tell Xinling, warning her about the vocational schools' exploitative practices. 'Ask yourself: Does the internship have any technical content? Is it relevant to the curriculum? The teachers don't think about these things at all, they just see the kids as fodder for the factories.' She desperately wanted a different future for her daughter.

In truth, Leiya and Chufeng thought their daughter was already much more intelligent than they had been at the same age. That was the case for all the kids in her generation: they had access to so much more information about the world from an earlier age thanks to the internet and their smartphones. But academic performance was all relative. Xinling was approximately twentieth in her fifty-student classroom. That sounded okay, but everyone knew the kids in the bottom ten slept through their lessons.

After the government had ordered schools to reduce academic pressure on children in the summer of 2021, Xinling's school had stopped officially announcing student rankings across her whole year group. But it didn't matter: everyone could guess their position anyway. Both students and parents remained invested in the rankings, since so much depended on them. And in their end-of-term exams, the students were still seated in blocks of fifty from the highest to the lowest scoring. Xinling worked out that she was also around 200th in her year of 500 students.

High schools recruit in the same way as universities: they take a fixed number of students each year, starting from the applicants with the top scores and going down the list. If next year's cohort is twice as clever as this year's, it doesn't matter: the same number will get into high school. The government maintains the target of having an equal proportion of sixteen-year-olds entering both the academic and vocational tracks. Xinling's middle school automatically admitted the top two hundred students in each year to its attached high school. The rest would have to look for other high schools – but the chance of entry was low, since those schools had even more competitive requirements.

Leiya had already worked so hard to secure Xinling a Shenzhen *hukou*, which gave her daughter an advantage over other migrant chidren without *hukou*. Those students, like her friend Yulan's daughter, would have 100 points automatically deducted from their *zhongkao* scores – roughly a fifth of the total points available – meaning they would need to perform much better than 'local' students to be admitted to the same high schools.

Leiya and Chufeng wanted Xinling to grasp the domino effect of every student's *zhongkao* exam performance. Education records went on to shape careers long after graduation. From the first day Chufeng worked in his government office, he understood that everyone's position depended on their schooling: high-school graduates, vocational college graduates like him, those with a bachelor's degree or a master's. The ranking determined your salary, pension and standing in the office.

———

A few evenings after the karaoke party, Leiya got into a fight with Xinling after school. Some parcels had arrived at their flat during the day.

'*Aiya*, you've bought new clothes again?' Leiya said.

'Can you pleeease not start on this again?' Xinling replied gently, drawing out her vowels.

Leiya blamed Xinling's interest in fashion, which she considered frivolous, for her lack of interest in school, but she also blamed herself for Xinling's middling academic performance. Maybe she hadn't spent enough time with her when she was little. Maybe she had been too busy working, putting her energy into supporting other mothers and their children. (Sometimes, when Leiya stayed late at the Banyan Tree Centre, Xinling would turn up and stride over to her mother, arm outstretched and finger pointed, and declare, 'We're going home!' Then she would turn on her heels and disappear.)

But Xinling was also highly driven outside of her studies in ways her mother didn't fully understand. She loved the arts, particularly music and dance. Her biggest regret this term was being taken off the school's cheerleading team because she couldn't do some of the moves. Now, every evening before she went to bed, she would press her feet against the frame of her bed and try to pull herself into the splits.

'Isn't that painful?' Leiya would ask, wincing as she watched.

'It has to be painful to work,' Xinling would reply.

Xinling competed in local dance competitions as well, for which she wore heavy stage make-up. Leiya was opposed to buying make-up and didn't wear it herself – she didn't think women needed it – so Xinling learned to apply it by watching her fellow dancers instead.

Xinling had once called her mother 'feudalistic' because of her opposition to buying make-up. She had used the word 'feudalistic' in the way that the Communist Party used the word shortly after they came to power in the 1949 revolution: to mean anything 'unmodern'. But in fact, the party had later denounced wearing make-up as a bourgeois fashion.

Xinling would convince Chufeng to buy her make-up since she knew Leiya wouldn't indulge her. *She really knows how to play us*, Leiya thought.

Leiya couldn't understand why Xinling was so obsessed with her appearance. Leiya had once bought her a top that Xinling said she couldn't wear because it was the wrong colour. One weekend, when they were walking in the alleyway and Leiya suggested they go to karaoke, Xinling turned round, went back home, and put on a whole new outfit. She often told Leiya she had no taste, but then she borrowed her mother's clothes, particularly her white trainers just after she'd scrubbed them clean. On their last parents' evening at school Xinling asked if Leiya was going to put on lipstick. The two of them were so different, Leiya sometimes felt like she didn't know whose belly her daughter had come from.

Then again, Leiya sometimes wondered what her life might have been like if she had been given the same opportunities as Xinling. She thought of her teenage self, the tall girl tugging at her too-short trousers, the one set of clothes she had to scrub for herself every weekend, too hungry to pay attention in class. She would smile, thinking that no matter the arguments she got into with her daughter about buying clothes, she was glad that Xinling had had a much better childhood.

At the very least, Xinling had never experienced the petty-minded patriarchy of the village, having grown up in the city. As a child, when people asked Xinling where she was from, she would naturally say she was from Lion's Head Village, the name of their urban settlement. But after she realised adults laughed at this reply, she became tongue-tied, unsure how to deal with the question. According to Chinese tradition, people are identified by their ancestral origins. The adults expected

Xinling to answer with the name of her mother or father's ancestral village, even though she herself had little memory of either place.

—

In Xinling's eyes, Leiya was loud, strict, often angry and, above all, very stingy. Xinling's great ambition, apart from winning a street-dance competition and making the cheerleading team, was to get rich. She had saved up for months to buy an electric piano that she could use to practise at home. Her mother understood why money was important to her, but it remained the source of many of their arguments.

For a while, Xinling jabbed at Leiya by complaining that the other kids in her class had access to after-school tutoring sessions, whereas Leiya was too frugal to buy her any.

Before the private education crackdown of summer 2021, there had been a floor filled with tutoring companies in the shopping mall near Xinling's school, and now there was just one left, which took advantage of the near-constant demand by hiking its prices. It was the only option, since Leiya didn't like the idea of buying classes online: how did you know you weren't getting scammed?

But Leiya felt bad about her arguments with Xinling over the classes. She went to the remaining education company, and talked them down from Rmb380 per hour to Rmb300 – more than what Leiya earned in a day at the factory. When she came home and offered the classes to Xinling, though, her daughter hesitated.

'It's too expensive,' Xinling said. 'Never mind.'

Leiya knew that, despite her provocations, Xinling understood the price of money. She also guessed that Xinling didn't want the added pressure of improving her grades in the wake of her mother's investment. Instead of after-school classes, Leiya found some older students in the neighbourhood, who charged only Rmb100 for an afternoon of one-to-one tuition. This was a good deal compared to the after-school classes, but they were often busy themselves, preparing for their university entrance exams.

Meanwhile, in the evenings, Xinling continued her stretching routine to prepare for her dance competitions and cheerleading try-outs. Sometimes Xinling would ask Leiya to help her, and Leiya would go along with it, bizarre as she found the exercises. She marvelled at her daughter. Even if it wasn't what she would have chosen, she had to admire the fact that Xinling was committed to something.

———

Xinling and Leiya often played out a pattern of defiance, confrontation, then truce. Leiya would start to monitor Xinling's homework for a while, then give up for another while, then revert. Both of them could see what was happening.

As the Labour Day school holidays approached in May, Leiya felt it was time for Xinling to buckle down and concentrate on her studies. She spent too much time playing on her phone, Leiya thought. Yes, she needed it to look things up, but then she would start messaging her friends and watching short video clips on Douyin. She got too easily distracted. She couldn't sit still for two hours, the typical length of an after-school class. Her grades were still middling.

On the first morning of the holidays, Leiya took away Xinling's phone. Xinling announced a hunger strike, but Leiya didn't relent.

In the evening, long after Leiya and Chufeng had eaten dinner, Xinling quietly put the kettle on and made herself instant noodles.

The next morning, when Leiya left the flat to go to the community centre, she felt the atmosphere was ripe for an explosion. Sure enough, a few hours later, her husband called her complaining that Xinling was refusing to go to the afternoon chemistry class they'd arranged for her.

Apparently Xinling had spent her morning sleeping in and lazing around, as was normal on a weekend, and he'd started chiding her to get up, but she'd not paid any attention. Leiya imagined the scene for herself: that over the course of the morning, his chiding had turned into scolding, and finally provoked an outburst from Xinling.

Next, she called her daughter.

'What's going on?' she asked.

'I don't want to study.'

'What would you rather do instead?'

'I'd rather die.'

Leiya got on her scooter immediately and went home, turning the situation over in her mind. She knew Xinling was under a huge amount of pressure at school. She knew she left the house at 7 a.m. and came back at 7 p.m., and spent the day being rushed from class to class, with not even the time to go to the toilet when she wanted. She knew Xinling was unhappy because of the phone incident, and on top of that, she thought, her husband had been his usual nitpicky and hot-tempered.

But to invoke suicide like this to your own mother was a sign of deep disrespect and, moreover, a threat, a way of abusively raising the stakes in an argument.

When Leiya got home, she took a knife from the kitchen and put it on the floor in front of Xinling, who was sulking in her bedroom.

'Do you really want to die?' Leiya said calmly. Xinling looked at the knife, and then back up at her mother. Leiya sensed something like regret in her gaze.

'Don't ever talk to me like that again,' Leiya said, more gently this time.

'Dad yelled at me all morning,' Xinling murmured.

'Your dad loves you with all his heart,' Leiya said. 'You know he's like that. He yells at both of us. He can't help it. He still loves you. He cooks three meals a day just how you like them. That's the way he expresses that he cares about you. You're the centre of the world in this house. We do everything we can for you. I know going to school is very hard. I know you're tired. I just want you to do well so you can have options.'

Next, she went to deal with Chufeng, who was sulking in their room. It was the Labour Day holiday, Leiya thought to herself, and she was spending it doing emotional labour – the hardest kind.

————

Sometimes Leiya's daughter would tell her that she'd earn money to look after her when she was old, and that Leiya would look after her kids in turn. She took for granted, of course, that she and her kids would be forever urban. These were throwaway remarks, a teenager playing grown-up.

But Leiya would tell Xinling that was not what she expected. After she had started volunteering for the City Workers' Community Centre all those years ago, she had been taught the importance of having social insurance; together with getting a city *hukou*, this meant she expected to receive a city pension.

She didn't need or want Xinling to support her financially in old age, she told her; she wanted her to live her life for herself.

242

'I can accept the idea of you never marrying, or never having kids, but I can't accept the idea of you not taking responsibility for yourself and for your kids, if you have them.'

Leiya saw this pattern too often: parents leaving their kids to be raised by the grandparents, absolving themselves of responsibility. She believed things turned out better for the kids if they were raised by their own parents. If you weren't prepared to do that, you shouldn't have kids, she thought. You shouldn't repeat the cycle of handing over responsibility to the older generation.

Her brother was a case in point: he and his wife hadn't prepared for their son's schooling, and waited too long to start working towards *hukou* or points-based school entry, meaning they had to spend upwards of Rmb10,000 a term on a private migrants' school. They couldn't keep this up indefinitely.

Leiya judged this whole issue to be her brother's problem. But now it had become her mother's. Her mother was getting ready to take her grandson back home, to the village she'd last lived in twenty years ago. It wouldn't be better for his education – the nearest school was still a long mountain trek away – but it would make ends meet more easily. And it would be tough for her, Leiya thought; she'd got used to the city, even its sticky, humid weather.

Leiya's mother was growing old in the city, but part of her wanted to go back, or perhaps wanted to be the kind of person who would want to go back, to be like the Chinese saying: fallen leaves return to their roots. She would keep putting off the decision. The kitchen roof on their old house had caved in and needed mending. When it was fixed, she'd go back.

When Leiya and her brother were teenagers, they had lived in that old house on their own. She still remembered the feeling of facing the world without a guardian. She was proud that through her efforts with her community centre and points-based school entry, she had created a novel way of keeping Xinling with her in the city. This was a privilege, for a migrant mother. Leiya's own mother, when working in the city, had never known of her teenage struggles back home. The arguments and the stress Xinling caused her were only possible because they were still together.

19

Revolutionaries at rest
Sam

As the disappearances of labour activists continued into the spring of 2019, Sam decided she had to move away from the city where the police were prowling.

Unlike many of the other students, she had her family to rely on; her parents, although they didn't fully understand what was going on, trusted her. They rented her a flat in their name a few hours away from Shenzhen, so she could stay there without being traced. She stopped using her old phone number. She told her friends she would be lying low for a while.

One rainy morning, Sam got up and noticed that her neighbour's window was open – strange, given the weather. Later that day, the electricity went out in her flat. Moments later, she heard a knock at the door, and a voice announcing, 'It's the property manager.' She opened it to find ten police officers standing outside. She later found they had been living in her neighbour's flat for the past few days, staking her out.

The 24-hour interrogation at the police station was relatively easy, in her view. She had not been a core part of the Jasic support group, after all. In the eyes of the police officers, she was a young girl led astray.

In the intervals between interrogations, she overheard police officers talking about her in the corridor outside the room.

'Who was that, the one who needed ten officers to bring her in?' asked one, sounding a mixture of shocked and impressed.

'Just some girl, a university student,' came the response. In her sleep-deprived state, Sam found this extremely funny. She would've laughed if she'd forgotten where she was.

Years later, Sam would act out this scene in front of her friends. 'Ten officers – all for me! They must have thought I was *fucking incredible*.'

———

The police released her without charge, then rang Sam's parents, who were extremely practical about the whole affair, all things considered. 'It is what it is,' her mother said.

Her father came to the police station to pick her up. He was angrier at the police than Sam was, complaining to the officers that they had detained his daughter for a day and night of intense questioning for nothing. Seeing her good-tempered father suddenly flare up, Sam started to wonder about an alternate reality in which he might have become a political radical himself. Then she put the thought aside, climbed into his car, and slept.

Back in Shenzhen, Sam allowed herself to rest for the first time in years. She spent nearly all her time at her parents' home, which suited her just fine. She was comfortable. When she started rereading her favourite texts – on Marx and Buddhism – it felt like reconnecting with old friends.

The police had warned her not to contact anyone affiliated with her old media outlet, Today's Collective, so she knew that her colleagues had likely been told not to contact her either. She fell out of touch with most of her former activist friends.

Now that she was prevented from doing any of her old work, at the age of twenty-seven Sam started having fun for the first time since she had embarked on her activist career. She was effectively out of a job, so her retired mother started taking her on tourist jaunts around Guangdong province. At home she watched television and enjoyed her parents' light-hearted banter. They had always got on well; their definitive sound was laughter.

Sam would joke that her greatest sacrifice while on the run was not being able to watch Real Madrid play. Back then, to protect her identity, she never used a SIM card registered to her own name, which was necessary to sign up for a wide range of services, including online TV streaming. Now she spent the summer watching football matches in the comfort of her family's living room.

Sam didn't think of her career so far as a sacrifice: it had never occurred to her she would do anything other than contribute to China's workers' movement in some way. But during the arrests of early 2019, she had felt more and more despair about what was happening in the wider movement. Her depression had ultimately been incapacitating, and stopped her from being further involved. Ironically, her depression may have protected her, by preventing her from becoming a more prominent political target.

When she tried to explain her feelings to her friends, she couldn't help but do so with her trademark sense of self-deprecation. Laughing at herself, she called her depression being 'lightly laden with grief', referencing the title of a Chinese novel. 'Sorry, I know it sounds dramatic. I'm not a dramatic person. It's just that dramatic things have happened to me.'

At the peak of the Jasic student disappearances, every time Sam sat down on her own she would feel the urge to cry. Now that she was back home, her despair hummed down to a low gloom. She started texting her old school friends again. She was a revolutionary at rest.

———

One day, after Sam had been home for about a month, four police officers came to her parents' flat and asked for her father by name, summoning him and Sam to the police station. They went, but her father was annoyed, and asked the police officers why they were making such a 'big deal' of things. The policemen looked surprised and crestfallen – they were used to having the family patriarch on their side, an ally who could rein in his rebellious daughter.

'She's been brainwashed by foreign forces,' the officers told her father. 'You haven't grasped the importance of this. What she's involved in is worse than killing ten or even a hundred people.' But Sam was never charged with any crime, and the officers couldn't go into more detail. It's possible that the local police, deputised by higher-up state security offices, actually had no idea about the specifics of Sam's involvement with the workers' movement.

On the way home, Sam chided her dad for being so stubborn in front of the officers. 'All they need is to be given some face. All you have to do is look solemn and nod,' she told him. 'It's all about letting them do their jobs and tick their boxes.'

Sam settled into a steady rhythm of meeting up with the police officer assigned to her case every couple of months. The first time he invited her out to lunch, Sam messaged back to ask if he would be paying. Yes, the officer replied. 'Can I bring my parents, then?' she asked. 'No, just yourself!' was the reply.

At lunch, the officer would ask about her plans, and mildly sing the praises of the Communist Party. He tried to win her over with assertions such as 'nobody in China lacks clothing or food', claims which she found laughable. She had a Chinese idiom for his wilful ignorance: 'Where your bum sits determines where your brain is.' But as she had advised her father to do, Sam would quietly listen and nod, devouring the Cantonese roasted pigeon that she ordered. These miniature birds were meant to be picked apart by hand; biting the caramelised skin off the bone required concentration. Later, her mother told her she should've asked for lobster.

When Sam's little sister was home during her high-school holidays, Sam joked that she could bring her along to one of these lunch meetings. She giggled to herself about her brazen opportunism, but ultimately decided not to push her luck.

The officer seemed greatly relieved when Sam told him that she was applying to PhD courses overseas. It meant that she wouldn't be his problem any more. 'If I get into a programme, you need to buy me lunch again to celebrate,' she quipped.

Going abroad to study was a choice many of Sam's activist friends had made, because leaving China meant getting a break from being harassed by the government. They saw it as an opportunity to recharge, reskill, and learn from movements abroad. For Sam, it was the natural extension of the desire to bury herself in books that she had had ever since her mother first took her to Shenzhen Children's Library as a preschooler.

She hadn't fully thought through how she could make her academic skills useful to the labour movement in China, and she feared being isolated from what was happening on the ground. But at present, she couldn't participate in any meaningful sense anyway, she reasoned, so she might as well learn something new.

Two years before, after the Jasic protests, all Sam could see were the problems facing the movement – problems she felt she needed to solve without knowing how. Now, she placed less of a burden on her own shoulders. She realised the movement's success was not entirely her responsibility. In retrospect, she saw that the secrecy of the student Maoist organisation had made it difficult for her to know who else she was working alongside, leaving her confused and isolated.

There was no good solution to this problem, she thought. A radical political organisation needed to protect its members through secrecy. But too much secrecy made everyone suspicious. Who decides who the comrades are, and who the opposition is? Who holds the power? At times Sam could sense the hidden decision-making apparatus behind the organisation, but it was always out of view.

She was wary of potential manipulation and domination of the mass movement by middle-class and elite participants. She knew that if she wanted to be a qualified organiser in the worker-and-peasant movement, she should lead a proletariat lifestyle, in the mode of the revolutionary leaders from the early days of the Communist Party. One such icon of hers, Peng Pai, was born to a wealthy landowning family, but publicly burnt his grandparents' wealth to demonstrate his commitment to the revolution.

To Sam, that was the level of transformation necessary to be a true organiser. But she also knew, and by this point accepted, that she would find it extremely hard to undertake it. The Foxconn recruiter who had refused her application to work there when she was a university student at the labour studies summer camp had been right: she was, indeed, a privileged urbanite who wouldn't have lasted long on the assembly line. Now she told her friends that she was fleeing to another university to continue to work and live as a middle-class intellectual.

———

Sam was ultimately accepted into a PhD programme abroad. Her parents were happy for her but not surprised – she had always excelled in school. She hadn't yet decided if she was going to commit to climbing the academic ladder abroad and to leave China for good. A large part of her felt the decision would depend on whether she liked the food.

While she had been on the run, during one of her bouts of depression, one anecdote had finally made her smile again. She had suddenly thought back to a friend of hers, who had described his experience studying abroad. Like her, he was from Guangdong, a province famed for its cuisine. One evening, while he was walking to the university canteen, thinking over in his head the different options for dinner, he burst into tears at the lack of good food to look forward to. Somehow this story had been the one thing to make her laugh during her torpid summer of depression after the Jasic arrests. And it was important to Sam that she retained her ability to laugh. It was often a choice between that or crying.

Sam started to make peace with her place in the movement. She wanted to contribute without driving herself back into a state of depression, which was, after all, ultimately counterproductive. She began more fully embracing her Buddhist as well as her Marxist beliefs: one preaches acceptance, and the other teaches the deterministic march of history. Whether you believed in it or not, she thought, the revolution would still come.

20

The New Year Festival
June

June finished her usual six-day week at the tech platform Paonow at 9 p.m. on a Saturday, the day before she was due to travel to her family home for the Chinese New Year holiday, the Spring Festival. She had been looking forward to the trip for a long time. Because of a mixture of Covid and short holidays, she'd missed the last Spring Festival, stranded in Beijing. This year, she ran the risk of stranding herself outside Beijing: clusters of infections popping up sporadically across the country, and if you were caught in one, you would be put into a local government quarantine centre. But June was determined to go home.

She boarded her flight wrapped in her black puffer jacket and a brown-and-cream-block woollen scarf. Without realising it, she had put on a similar outfit to the one her sister had worn on her first trip home from the city, flush with factory wages and city fashions: knee-high black leather boots, flesh-coloured tights. June liked black; she felt it was a mature colour. She had sworn off pink because it was for teenage girls.

She spent the two-hour flight dozing and daydreaming about the food that awaited her. June's father had recovered from his stabbing over a decade ago, except for a weak right arm, and could tend his land. Every autumn, he picked her favourite variety of wild mushroom when they bloomed in the mulch of the mountainside for a few brief weeks. This year, he had frozen them for her return, now and then shooing away other family members from opening the pack.

After a day's travel, she arrived in her county town in the late evening, dumped out of the bus onto a street that she didn't immediately recognise. It had been resurfaced and redecorated since she had last visited, and its trees sparkled with red Spring Festival lights. The snow was coming down lightly in wet flakes. Her sister May pulled up, and she climbed into the car. May's preschool daughter clung to her aunt.

The last time June had gone home was for May's wedding two years ago. When she was growing up, she hadn't regarded the mountain landscape with much significance; on her long walks to and from school, she mostly wished that her home was a little closer.

But that spring, the mountains were filled with alpine flowers and, after years away in the city, June suddenly found it all vividly beautiful. It was as if she were seeing her home through Teacher Song's foreign eyes for the first time. It was so quiet that you could sleep as late as you wanted, cradled in the mountains. It was the kind of place people from Beijing would go on holiday, June realised.

———

The first night of the New Year holiday, June stayed with May in her new flat in the county town. May had renovated it to her own taste, with grey marble-effect floors and sky-blue curtains framing the floor-to-ceiling windows, from which one could see the snow-streaked mountains.

A few years ago, the local government had offered June's neighbours in her village the option of moving into a block of newly built resettlement apartments in the town. By then, May had already bought her first town apartment, and thus wasn't eligible for the government's offer. Her neighbours had initially been hesitant. Accepting the deal included demolishing their old homes. May's cousin decided to try it out: she was already working in the county town, so would have to buy eventually. Their older relatives, however, stayed put in their village homes. At least they'd had the choice: in many other regions, local governments had forced farmers to move in order to meet their urbanisation targets.

After the cousin moved into her new apartment, May's grandmother visited and looked out from its sixth-floor window at the town skyline of roads and high-rises.

'This is boring,' she declared. She and May's father worried about getting lost in the town's streets, unable to read its signs. Moreover, there was nothing for them to do in an apartment hoisted several storeys above the earth. There was no land to farm, and nothing else they thought they could offer the town to make a living.

May kept driving her grandma and father into the town on odd weekends to acquaint them with her life, with the town's restaurants, with how easy it was to keep a place clean when you lived in an apartment rather than a farmhouse. Seeing May's newly renovated second apartment, her grandma had to admit she was impressed. She said that it made her own house look like a pigsty.

——

On the morning of Chinese New Year's Eve, June set off with May, her niece and her brother-in-law, who drove them along the single-track road into the snowy mountains. At the top of the ridge that ran down to June's hamlet, she stopped to take photos. Below was a sweep of snowy valley, and amid the white was a patchwork field of tender greens and yellows, the rapeseed plants and cabbages that grew all winter. They drove along the road that May and her cousin had first carved into a path with the adults of their village in the early 2000s. The government later widened it into a cement road. Before her mother's death, their family was one of the first in the village to build a new brick house by the road. One by one, other families moved their homes up to be near the planned path of the new road. By the time June went to university, the road was completed.

After that, developments accelerated, spurred by the government's flagship Targeted Poverty Alleviation policy. When June came back from her first year of university, there were street lamps dotting the road; after her second year, her home had an internet connection.

But what stunned her most was the water tap that was installed during her third year of university. From the age of four, June had spent hours each week bringing water to the house, carrying on her soft shoulders a pole with a bottle swinging from each end. The sway of the bottles unbalanced her, and she couldn't hold her core stiffly enough to resist being thrown from side to side as she walked. Her grandma had told her to marry into a family that lived nearby so that, in his old age, her father would find it easier to fetch water for June.

The tap was installed on the outside of their house, facing the street to allow passers-by to help themselves. The first time June saw it, she twisted it open, sending a jet of water into the earth below. She cupped her hands under it: the high pressure felt astonishing. She stared at the gushing tap for some time, marvelling at how much her home had changed, until her father came out and told her to turn it off.

———

Like many rural houses, June's was carefully covered in white tile. By the front door, a local-government-issued banner made of sun-faded red fabric proclaimed the family a 'Clean and Civilised Household'. Underneath it was an old piece of paper with the words of the 'Targeted Poverty Alleviation Educational Subsidies Song', whose rhymes were written for the local dialect:

> *Attend upper-secondary, enjoy three years of subsidies*
> *Attend vocational school, enjoy two years of subsidies*
> *Every student every year one thousand renminbi*
> *Plus an extra 'double subsidy':*
> *Textbooks four hundred yuan*
> *Five hundred yuan for dormitory fees*
> *Studying is good, and by no means lazy*
> *The subsidy policy warms our hearts*
>
> *Whether university or vocational college,*
> *Annual subsidy over four thousand in total*
> *Every student every year one thousand renminbi*
> *Plus university gets you an extra 3,830*
> *Vocational college gets you an extra 3,500*
> *If you study, you must focus*
> *The party's kindness is like a warm spring breeze*

Inside the entrance room of the house was a shrine to the family's ancestors. The doors opening to the side rooms were still covered in primary-school certificates that June had won over a decade ago, although their golden lettering remained bright.

Indoors, June's breath condensed into white clouds and mingled with the smoke from the wood fire. Everyone kept their down jackets on. Once the family was assembled, they started preparing the main meal of the day. First, June's grandma rang the silver bell on the shrine three times, calling the ancestors to eat. On the table below the shrine, she set out a pot filled with meat and soup. Around the pot, she set the table with bowls and chopsticks, kumquats and red cans of sugary tea.

For the living, May boiled the shrimp, fried smoked meat with spring onions, and prepared ingredients for the hotpot: marinated beef offal and tender piles of fluffy beansprouts. Finally, the wild mushrooms that June had been waiting to eat since October were boiled in a clear broth with the freshly slaughtered chicken.

When the meal was almost ready, June's father dispatched her to fetch her uncle from his house down the hill. June felt unsteady going down the slope, the heels of her leather city boots landing at odd angles on the uneven concrete. Behind her were the mountains she had scrambled up as a child, scavenging for wood to heat her primary-school classroom.

As she and her uncle walked back, May's husband came outside and unfurled a string of red firecrackers a few metres in front of the house. May gathered the children together and gave them yellow joss paper to burn for the ancestors. When the papers finished burning, everyone went back inside, save May's husband, who lit the end of the chain of firecrackers, then sprinted back into the house. The sound exploded in their eardrums; a car alarm went off in the distance. 'Time to eat!' he yelled, and everyone settled around the table for the New Year's Eve feast.

———

The next morning, June's grandma looked out onto the road strewn with the wet paper shrapnel of red firecrackers and saw that May's husband's car was no longer parked outside.

'Did you have a fight last night?' she asked her.

No, May replied, he'd simply parked behind the house to avoid the firecrackers. Her grandma couldn't read words, but she read people with great vigilance. Once, when May had brought home some sour passion fruit, a fruit rarely seen in those parts, her grandma had asked her if her taste for strong flavours meant she was pregnant. When May eventually did become pregnant with her daughter, she was living in her factory's dormitories near Shanghai. Her grandma had been too far away to read the signs.

The first day of Chinese New Year is for resting. Nobody goes anywhere. June's relatives played round after round of mah-jong. Every now and then, a stray burst of firecrackers would cut the conversation. Fields have to lay fallow, and humans do too. In the farmland, winter forces rest. In a city, one easily forgets to.

Later that day, June received an urgent request from her boss to compile a series of market-research spreadsheets on what products were sold at high frequency on competitors' platforms and at what price. The goal was to help new shops participating in Paonow's grocery-delivery expansion select stock to sell. He sent her a WeChat red envelope with digital money by way of apology.

The next day, June got up before dawn to make a dent in her work. Then she set off in the mid-afternoon to visit her maternal grandparents' family, as is customary on the second day of New Year. The itinerary was three rounds of dinner at three different houses. She took her laptop with her, hoping for some time to sneak in a bit of work.

At the first house, June and her sister arrived just as the grandparents were bringing a herd of yellow buffalo up to the stables behind the house. Inside the house was a teenage boy, June's cousin, filling in a multiple-choice test in his literature textbook in preparation for his *gaokao* exams. His grandparents joked good-naturedly about how he was bound to outdo everyone else in the family except June.

'You'll be fine,' June said. 'We've got good genes, right?' Another cousin had just been admitted to a good university the previous year.

Their older cousins were there, too. One of them, Kangfu, wore a black beanie hat over his buzz-cut hair, printed with the slogan 'Temperature Normal'. The phrase had become ubiquitous during the pandemic, blurted out by temperature-scanning infrared cameras in shopping malls. June remarked to everyone that she and Kangfu had been in the same year in middle school, and that his grades had been much better than hers at the time.

'Want to know where it all went wrong?' Kangfu said, grinning to the assembled audience. 'Young love,' he said. 'I was twelve or thirteen. She was in my class. We didn't learn a thing after that.' All the relatives were chuckling. Kangfu put his bowl down on the floor to count on his fingers. 'Now, she's my ex-ex-ex-ex-ex . . .'

Everyone laughed again. May and June smiled along; they knew Kangfu was joking. Maybe it had been young love that had ended his progress. But most likely it was the accident he had at the age of sixteen when he was bringing the family buffalo home. He was hospitalised for much of the rest of the school year, and by the time he was out, he didn't have the money to repeat his classes. He moved to the city to work on a construction site with his older cousin.

The children of the village were more likely to follow Kangfu's path than June's. When May came across kids left to take care of themselves, kids who were a head or so shorter than the city kids the same age, she would think to herself: these are the ones who will go out and do hard labour.

She thought this with exasperation rather than judgement. She herself hadn't gone to high school, and had gone to work in garment factories from the age of sixteen.

Through her factory work, May had funded June through high school, which had enabled her to go on to university; now June was earning enough money to send some back home. May had eventually got high-school qualifications by taking a part-time adult education course, escaped the assembly line and landed an office job.

They were still a family of daughters, with no sons, but the other villagers no longer bullied them for this. Instead, they held them in high esteem: they knew May was making a good life for herself, and while nobody understood exactly what June did, they all knew she had done well at school and was now living in the capital. The villagers all agreed that the family's ancestors were looking after them well.

Epilogue

In the winter at the end of 2021, I suggested to Dan, the friend I had met at a rooftop party shortly after arriving in Beijing, that we go back to our home province of Sichuan together. I wanted to see my grandparents, and Dan wanted to see her grandmother too, as she had recently moved into a new apartment built by the local government. This was a big move for her: after she married at the age of twenty, and up to the age of seventy, she had lived in the same farmhouse.

In the 1960s, Dan's grandmother Yubin had given birth to all four of her children in that farmhouse. For her first child, she had the help of a midwife, as she did for her second child, Dan's mother. By the time it came to her third and fourth children, she was so well practised that she cut their umbilical cords herself with a pair of embroidery scissors. After staying indoors for the traditional month of postnatal rest, she was back in the fields.

When the local government demolished the farmhouse in the late 2010s as part of its urbanisation drive, Dan's grandma moved to Shenzhen to live with Dan's parents while waiting for the government to build their new resettlement apartments. This gap of having nowhere to live posed a problem for some of the farmers who were both lucky and unfortunate enough to give their homes away in a forced exchange of riches. Yubin's village, like others across the country, was split between those who vehemently opposed demolition and wanted to remain in their homes, and those who preferred cashing in and having a new life in the city.

Dan drove me and my grandparents to visit Yubin in her new apartment. I followed her into the entrance of a large, gated compound. Huge woven straw mats covered the road in front of the gates. Lying on top of the mats to sun-dry were red adzuki beans, chestnuts and other early-winter harvests. A few dried corn cobs, emptied of their teeth, were strewn on the pavement. The tarmac had covered the farmland, but the farmland had come out on top.

We picked up Yubin and took a short drive to the site where her village had once stood: Dan wanted to show it to me. We entered a narrow road that cleaved into a vast expanse of demolished countryside, the dug-up rust-coloured soil covered with the green plastic netting that signals construction in progress. Except nothing had progressed for two years. The demolitions had started just before the arrival of Covid, which paused many construction projects.

At the top of the hill stood a handful of old courtyard houses, the remainder of Yubin's village.

The roofs of the houses were traditional rows of clay tiles, covered in a thick layer of dried leaves and twigs. A shop's shutters were pulled down; metal gates were locked. But the fields around the buildings were planted with rows of giant, sun-devouring cabbages and pea shoots, all the glorious shades of green. Sycamore saplings had sprung up in the long grass by the roadside.

Adverts were stencilled onto the walls of the buildings:

Hong's agency: marriage introductions, job introductions, second-hand cars.

Bank loans: business loans, social-security payment loans, agricultural loans, use your house as guarantee.

Tacked on the wall of a closed-down convenience store was a poster showing a new planned development: 'Elegant Gaoyuan. Our common home.' It bore an illustration of white fifteen-storey shafts rising in a neat grid along a six-lane road dotted with cars.

Yubin wandered down the road towards a sign that said, in clumsily aerosol-sprayed yellow letters, 'Junk Recycling'. She turned into a courtyard to find an island of life in the emptied village. Under the awning of the courtyard roof were two tables of elderly people playing cards, their hands holding the Sichuanese variety that are long and thin, like bookmarks. Small piles of pebbles marked each player's wins, polished by passing through so many pairs of warm hands. They were living in the few houses that had been left behind, their demolition halted by the pandemic.

'Ah, you're here,' said one of the women, making room for Yubin to sit down at her table. She carried on playing cards, as if nothing was out of the ordinary, as if Yubin came by every day rather than once a year. Life in the village was always like this: departures were followed by arrivals and yet more departures.

——

Like others all over China, the local government in Dan's home town was demolishing villages in order to force the advent of urbanisation. In 2013, Xi Jinping's first year in power, just over half of Chinese people lived in towns and cities. The government set a goal of increasing that to 60 per cent, meaning moving a further 100 million rural residents into newly created towns and cities by 2020.

There was a second reason behind the demolitions: local governments rely on land sales for revenue. Spending on construction and infrastructure boosts land prices and is the easiest way for officials to skim off some of the fat from procurement contracts.

The local government in Dan's home town had a further goal: to build a tourist attraction by its vast lake to cater for urban families from the provincial capital of Chengdu.

After we finished looking around the demolished village, Dan drove Yubin, my grandparents and me to the new 'eco-park' nearby.

We drove through a manicured expanse that spread like the estate of an absent duke. It was populated mostly with gardeners, who were hosing the thirsty green lawns. Trees and bushes stood wrapped in translucent sheets of plastic, as if newly bought gifts from the store. The layers protected them from the Sichuanese winter, a gardener told us.

We tried aimlessly to find a path. We walked past a large advert whose half-fallen canvas revealed the vision for the park: two blonde-haired children running in a field of grass.

Let your children's footprints slowly grow by the lakeside.
Children have their futures, they will fly above the lake's
surface, they will swim in the air. Before that time comes,
let the moment linger a little on this lakeside.

We walked past the humming air vents of a newly opened Intercontinental hotel, its glass façade dominating the scenery. We walked on past a basketball court, a tennis court, a series of open invitations to a future that hadn't yet arrived.

Before my parents took me to the UK at the age of four, I lived near the Emei River with my grandparents and great-grandma. Now whenever I visit, every morning I wander by the riverbank, mesmerised by Sichuan's characteristic mist, how it obscures and gives depth, and how it layers the mountains in the near and far distance into the suggestive blue-grey shadows of a traditional Chinese watercolour painting.

On a clear day one can see the arch of Emei Mountain, whose name means 'eyebrow'. The riverbank is densely fringed with trees and thickets of bamboo grown so bushy that their heads droop down like green dragons bowing. When I was little, this was a muddy path that we would walk to get into town. It is now paved, but the greenery remains.

Every time I visit, I am dazzled by the vibrant greens of the vegetables that the farmers grow by the riverside, the monstrously giant cabbages that bloom in Sichuan's rust-red soil and mild, humid climate. The province is known as Heaven's Granary. Because of all this agriculture and old forest, the river's bank has escaped the cement encroachment of larger towns.

The Emei River flows down from the 3,100-metre-high reaches of Emei Mountain, past my grandparents' village, into a natural swimming pool carved into the riverside by the locals. Then it winds past farmers' houses, preserved with their original courtyard walls and their roofs of curved tiles stacked in rows like fish scales. Banyan trees cover the homes with their dark, glossy canopies.

Then the river flows into Emei town, where its banks become paved and lined with street markets frequented by the elderly, selling everything from floral-patterned vest jackets to Mao-era memorabilia badges and propaganda posters. It continues eastwards to the city of Leshan, famous for the Giant Buddha carved into the red rock face of a mountainside; in 2020, the river flooded to lap at the Buddha's feet.

In Leshan, the Emei River blends with other tributaries to become the Yangtze River, known in Chinese as the Changjiang, or 'long river'. It continues eastwards for hundreds of miles before arriving in Shanghai and flowing into the Pacific Ocean. The molecules of my home town and Dan's diffuse across the earth and return in the snow that falls each year on Mount Emei's summit.

––––

Dan drove me to Emei, and I took her to the old block of flats where I had once lived with my grandparents as a toddler. Whenever I visit, I try to find time to walk up the hill to these old apartments, just to look at their mould-stained façades. My grandma sees my routine of visiting the old apartment as proof of my filial devotion, because it signified my nostalgia for the childhood we spent together. To me, my attachment to the old block of flats was simple: it was the only place in the world I knew that had barely changed since I was little.

Between all my parents' moves around the UK, I visited my grandparents whenever we could afford the plane fare, which worked out to be almost every other summer holiday. My grandparents lived in the same apartment from the time my mother started middle school to the time I started university.

In the summers when I visited, I slept on a bed with a top sheet made of glossy slats of bamboo for keeping cool. My pillow was covered with a pink towel embroidered in red flowers to wick the sweat from our necks.

I was disappointed when I heard my grandparents were moving into a newer residential compound their *danwei* had built for them further downhill, closer to the city centre.

I knew it was for their convenience: it was the first place they had lived with running hot water.

The cold mist descended again the afternoon that Dan and I walked up to the Buddhist temples at the foot of Emei Mountain. A stone path took us uphill through the forest, winding around 700-year-old trees, their bark dark with damp: cedars, giant redwoods. In the first century CE, the first Buddhist temple in China was built at the summit of Emei Mountain. The summit remains a pilgrimage site, particularly for nuns. All the way from the foot to the summit stand monasteries from various centuries, serving vegetarian food and housing walkers for overnight stays.

I can't recall if the paved stone tourist paths were built in my early twenties, or if that was just when I started to develop a memory for the paths winding up through the mountainside, the time I started to map my own routes for myself. I have brought many friends from far afield to walk it with me.

All these different visitors came to mind as Dan and I sat on a stone bench by the Emei River at the foot of the mountain. Just around this bend of the river, on the other side of the bank, was a small farmer's restaurant that served tofu freshly made from the mountain spring water. It was the same bench, the same view that I'd seen on several such walks over the past decade.

It seemed to me suddenly miraculous that I was first an infant here, trailing after my family, then returned as an adult, able to choose my own paths.

I tried to express this feeling to Dan.

'You're so lucky that your childhood hasn't been demolished,' she replied. 'If this were my home town, I'd come back all the time.'

In the last days of 2022, eight months after I had moved back to the UK, the Chinese government suddenly lifted all of its pandemic restrictions, and its borders lay gaping open after three years of being bound shut.

In the spring of 2023, I went back to China: something I thought I wouldn't be able to do for a long time. During my pandemic years in Beijing, I started dreaming that I had accidentally slipped over the border and was stuck outside the mainland. Now, the portal between the two worlds was open again.

Distance matters for security: communicating with interviewees online is nearly always vulnerable to surveillance. While I was writing this book, I feared that not getting back into China meant never being able to speak to my interviewees again. We can never predict what political winds might change to make some previously safe topic politically sensitive.

I saw Dan, who was successfully resisting her parents' attempts to set her up with various sons of neighbours and was now studying to become a lawyer. She was inspired to do so after becoming her office's confidante for relationship troubles – a natural role for her, given her fascination with trying to see the different points of view in people's intimate lives – and realising how much legal procedure there is in a divorce.

Siyue and Benji had managed to turn their company around in a phenomenal way, escaping the destruction of the private education industry. Siyue had lost some of her drive for entrepreneurship, but was excited about travelling abroad again, as doing so had always brought her inspiration.

June was by far the busiest: she had left her job at the online delivery services company in order to start up her own firm.

She was working the hardest she ever had in her life, not stopping for holidays or weekends. She had barely taken a break for Chinese New Year.

Leiya's community centre, to my surprise, was still going strong, with a fresh batch of funding from a local charitable foundation. She was still working full-time at the electronics factory. To her relief, her daughter Xinling got into a decent high school.

Sam had completed the first year of her PhD. The food abroad, she said, is edible.

————

At the time of this writing in the summer of 2023, the Chinese economy is slowing down. Such a slowdown is inevitable for a country that had been growing at breakneck speed. The incredible rate of growth in the 1980s introduced an unprecedented level of social mobility by lifting people out of almost uniform poverty. Now, class inequalities have set in once more, and the inevitable economic slowdown means it is harder to achieve any kind of mobility unless structural impediments and injustices are addressed.

Since the pandemic, youth unemployment rates are over 20 per cent, making it much more difficult for the next cohort of Junes and Siyues to leave their villages and gain footholds in the city. The global economy outside China is not faring much better, either. Despite these challenges, what I felt from all my friends and interviewees in China was the determination to adapt to the unpredictability of life. When I talk to them about my fear that China might become ever more closed to the outside world, some reassure me that while China's changing political sensitivities might be hard to predict, so too are the long-term political outcomes for the country.

Up to now, it has seemed unlikely that the government would or could address many of the roots of social immobility that this book explores: the *hukou* system, the deep inequalities in education and health-care provision, the exploitative nature of the low-waged manufacturing and service sectors. Simpler problems than these afflict much richer countries with longer-established political institutions – not least my own, the UK. Governments are easily trapped in cycles where a minority with vested interests successfully defend their power at the expense of the majority of the population, delaying long-needed reforms. As a result, in China and elsewhere, land and other resources are hoarded and used ineffectively. Unfair advantages, like tax breaks and *hukou* privileges, are held on to by the wealthiest. Political attention is given to those with access to power, rather than those who most need change.

While I remain hopeful that the future might bring fresh solutions, many possibilities have already been closed for some of those living in the present – particularly migrant and casual workers, like Leiya's friends.

Leiya, Dan, Siyue, June and Sam are all unusually accomplished idealists; if they weren't, they wouldn't have tried to do improbable things. They are open to new ideas and self-transformation; they reflect deeply and face their challenges, while also finding resilience through their loving interdependence with family and friends.

They demonstrate the creative ability of humans to transform themselves, and to make possible what was previously unimaginable – particularly when in supportive, like-minded communities. I have a feeling they will surprise us yet. Perhaps they will find ways of staying in the city; perhaps they will choose to leave on their own terms, and make better lives elsewhere.

The Buddhists of Emei Mountain are right that the only constant in life is change. Who, a century ago at the founding of China's Communist Party, could have predicted the revolution of 1949? Who, barely thirty years later, could have predicted the Reform era?

———

One morning in the autumn of 1949, my grandfather, then ten years old, opened the front gate of his mother's courtyard to see some sixty men sleeping on the pavement outside.

There was a chill in the early-morning air; the men slept on thin bedrolls. They were wearing khaki uniforms, and were soldiers from the Communist Party's army who had quietly arrived in the riverside Sichuanese town of Hejiang overnight.

My grandfather told his parents what he saw, and they were stunned. When the soldiers of the ruling Kuomintang army had come into town, they had caused havoc, commandeering schools and houses for their soldiers to stay in. Now the Communists had arrived with barely a sound, their men sleeping on the ground, covering the streets.

The Kuomintang had fled Hejiang. The Communists had taken it without a fight: a silent revolution, overnight.

References and further reading

Siyue

Charlotte Brontë, *Jane Eyre*. Originally published in 1847.

Deborah Carlisle Solomon, *Baby Knows Best: Raising a Confident and Resourceful Child, the RIE Way*, Little, Brown & Company, 2014.

Jane Nelsen, Cheryl Erwin and Roslyn Duffy, *Positive Discipline: The First Three Years*. Originally published in 1998.

June

Scott Rozelle and Natalie Hell, *Invisible China: How the Urban-Rural Divide Threatens China's Rise*, University of Chicago Press, 2022.

San Mao, *Stories of the Sahara*, translated by Mike Fu, Bloomsbury Publishing, 2020.

American Dreams in China (film), released 2013.

Leiya

Eli Friedman, *The Politics of Development, Labor Markets, and Schooling in the Chinese City*, Columbia University Press, 2022.

Diana Fu, *Mobilizing Without the Masses: Control and Contention in China*, Cambridge University Press, 2017.

Pun Ngai, *Made in China: Women Factory Workers in a Global Workplace*, Duke University Press, 2015.

Sam

Joel Andreas, *Disenfranchised: The Rise and Fall of Industrial Citizenship in China*, Oxford University Press, 2019.

Jenny Chan, Mark Selden and Pun Ngai, *Dying for an iPhone: Apple, Foxconn and the Lives of China's Workers*, Pluto Press, 2020.

Ching Kwan Lee, *Against the Law: Labor Protests in China's Rustbelt and Sunbelt*, University of California Press, 2007.

Index

democracy, 71, 123, 126, 181
Deng Xiaoping, xi, 63, 65, 71,
    74–5, 126
Dewey Decimal System, 145
Didi ride-hailing app,
    86, 212–16
Discovery Channel, 70
Disneyland Shanghai, 115
divorce, 178
Douyin app, 80, 217, 240
dowries, 108

E
early-childhood
    development, 229–30
economic slowdown, 269
education
    adult education, 93, 151, 260
    compulsory system, 28–9, 153
    double reduction policy, 195
    early childhood
        education, 168–9
    girls' education, 34–5
    holistic education, 13,
        222, 224
    inequalities in, 270
    international teaching
        styles, 138–9
    jiwa (pressure on
        children), 82
    neijuan ('involuted'), 82
    online education, 82
    physical education, 46, 79
    private education and
        tutoring, 47–9, 56, 91–2,

78–80, 96, 136–47, 195–6,
    220–2, 224–5, 227–8,
    239–40
see also schools; universities
Education Bureau, 10–11
education tech sector, 82–90
electricity, 8, 65
Emei Mountain, xii, xv, 265,
    267, 271
Emei River, 265–7
English language, 12, 17–18,
    27, 45–7, 57, 93–100,
    131, 134, 136–8, 142, 203,
    221–2, 227
English Premier League, 67
Enjoy English camps, 93–4
Evergrande, 199–200

F
factory work, 29–30, 40–3,
    101–2, 106, 153–60, 209,
    211–12, 260
    factory relocations, 153–4,
        205
    increased surveillance, 157
    injuries and suicide, 115–20
    job adverts, 211
    and vocational
        schools, 233–5
    see also Foxconn; Jasic;
        labour organisation;
        shipyard workers
fake identity certificates, 39–40
Falun Gong, 72–3
family counselling, 222

276

Acknowledgements

Above all, my thanks for this book go to Siyue, June, Leiya, Sam and Dan for inspiring me with their lives, and to their mothers and grandmothers for sharing their homes and stories with me. Thanks go also to the dozens of other interviewees who took risks by sharing their accounts. Thank you to the feminist teacher Feng Yuan, the inspirational Teresa Xu, the labour sociologist Jenny Chan, as well as the many activists, journalists and academics in China who have taught me so much, but who I cannot name.

Thank you to my parents and my maternal grandparents for entertaining my unending questions from the day I learned how to say them, and for being willing to share stories from decades past at the drop of a hat.

Thank you to my many teachers across my many primary schools, who were patient with a non-English-speaking child. Thank you to my early friends, teachers and mentors who saw me as a writer: Frances Edwards, Jannat Hossain, Stephen Brown, Danny Broderick and Steve Dearden from The Writing Squad, Jacob Sam-La Rose of the Barbican Young Poets, and Stuart Silver of Spread The Word x The London Laureates.

I started taking myself as seriously as a first-time author partly as a result of the encouragement of Julian Gewirtz, the world's best pep-talker. Eli Friedman imparted his confidence in my project as well as his expertise on labour issues. Thomas Graziani gave me exactly the support I needed while writing, and read all of my early drafts. My agents, Matthew Marland and Alice Whitwham, were the best I could ask for, and have vastly improved the book. I am so glad to have been published by Jasmine Horsey, Lindsey Schwoeri and Allie Merola, who are not only incisive and thoughtful in their edits but also have been wonderful to work with from start to end. I feel I've been unusually lucky with my whole team.

My editors at the *Financial Times* gave me a year away from my reporting job to write this book. Thanks go to Jamil Anderlini and Tom Mitchell for bringing me on board this wonderful newspaper eight years ago. I have had so many mentors there: in particular, Robin Kwong, who gave generously of his time and advice when I most needed it as a new reporter; Malcolm Moore, who always knows what to say in every situation; James Kynge, the wisest sage of China reporting; Alec Russell, who commissioned my first long-form essays and enabled me to flourish; Lionel Barber, who was crucial in urging me onwards with this book; and Roula Khalaf, who has helped me feel seen, valued and supported.

My thanks finally go to all those who filled my six years in Beijing with joy and care, and taught me more about the vast country that I only comprehend a little of: Nian Liu, Qianer Liu, Sue-Lin Wong, Emily Feng, Ryan McMorrow, Sun Yu, Ginny Ge and all the staff of the *FT* Beijing bureau; Melody Lin, who fact-checked parts of this book; my fellow travellers Patrick Baert, David Rennie and Jiehao Chen; Feifei Lu, Lysa, Ivy, Xiao Xiong, Songqiao, Xu, Lesli and Juli. And, of course, thanks to Haohao, who still walks by my side.